PETER JACKSON
IN PERSPECTIVE

S. Cip
11/3/05

PETER JACKSON
IN PERSPECTIVE

THE POWER BEHIND CINEMA'S
THE LORD OF THE RINGS

A Look at Hollywood's Take on
Tolkien's Epic Tale

GREG WRIGHT

With Foreword By
DAVID BRUCE

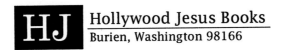

HJ Hollywood Jesus Books
Burien, Washington 98166

Library of Congress Control Number: 2004111035

Cover Photo by Ana Elisa Fuentes / Getty Images.

Hollywood Jesus Books is an independent and authorized print publisher for writers published online by:
                    http://www.hollywoodjesus.com

For My Elven Ladies: Wendi, Jessi, Emily and Julia

Long not for the past, nor to master all the tides of the world—
but to fulfill the promise of the future.

Acknowledgments

I am deeply indebted to David Bruce, webmaster and creator of Hollywood Jesus, for the opportunity I've had over the last several years to write a lengthy series of articles on Peter Jackson's films. I have been privileged to participate, in some small way, in the cultural phenomenon that *The Lord of the Rings* has become. I am also grateful for the long patience of Ted Gartner at Grace Hill Media, and his willingness to humor me in my rather anxious pursuit of inside information from New Line Cinema.

Credit is also due to my editors at Hollywood Jesus—to my wife, Jenn, for serving faithfully on the front lines, and to Lyn Mellone, for giving the website an eleventh-hour going-over with a fine-tooth comb. My father may be right that the devil is in the details. Thanks to him, also, for understanding when my life took this unexpected turn away from the pastoral ministry we shared.

A huge thanks also to Mike Perry at Inkling Books for his encouragement to proceed with this project, and for the tremendous resource he has been in bringing it to fruition. Thanks also go to James Harleman at Seattle's Mars Hill Church and Mike Gunn at Harambee Church for opportunities to develop challenging lectures based on Jackson's films. In addition, it has been a pleasure working with Ron Cleveland, principal organizer of RingCon, the Pacific Northwest's biannual Tolkien convention.

Finally, many thanks to the host of Tolkien and Jackson fans who, over the years at Hollywood Jesus, have helped to keep me honest. Your e-mails have been my constant companions, and I am grateful for the many friendships I have formed through them. Thank you Janet, Jeremy, Mark, Brian, Loren, and Henk, among many others. Iron does indeed sharpen iron. I hope—nay, expect—that we shall all meet someday.

Contents

Foreword

Art often takes on a life of its own, achieving far more than the artist could have imagined. This tendency is certainly true of *The Lord of the Rings*—both the unparalleled novel by J. R. R. Tolkien and the films of Peter Jackson.

Keir Dullea, who played one of the leads in *2001: A Space Odyssey*, attributed the immense popularity of that film to the universal sense of wonder it induced: "not only our wonder about space, but our wonder about time, our wonder with our relationship to the Deity perhaps—because you get as many interpretations of what the film means as you do people who have seen it." And the wonder of *2001: A Space Odyssey* succeeded in becoming indelibly imprinted on the public imagination not just because of the original book by Arthur C. Clarke but because of the genius of master filmmaker Stanley Kubrick as well.

Peter Jackson has accomplished a remarkably similar feat. He has interacted with J. R. R. Tolkien's legendary material in such a profound manner as to produce a cinematic masterpiece that has resonated powerfully in the minds of moviegoers worldwide. Few Hollywood directors have risen to the level of Kubrick—you can count them on one hand—and Peter Jackson just happens to be one of them. *The Fellowship of the Ring*, *The Two Towers* and *The Return of the King* are among the highest-grossing films of all time, and are now included in the top ten of IMDb's All-Time Worldwide Boxoffice list.

Peter Jackson is the kind of artist that Shira P. White writes

1

about in *New Ideas about New Ideas*: "Creative people tend to have a heightened sensitivity to intricacy, subtlety, and nuance. They have a superior capacity to sense, process, and find value in quiet, tangential, and distant beeps, blips and flashes. Expanding our consciousness to take in more diverse and faint tickles and proddings…" His creativity is coupled with a perfectionism that demands countless takes of every scene. He insists on special effects that are seamless and invisible. Yet in terms of production values, he has always brought his pictures in for less money than his peers.

His creativeness is also tied to his spirituality. A theologian he is not. However, he knows how to intrinsically connect stories to the deep inner spiritual longings and sensibilities of people worldwide. It is on this level that I find Jackson so intriguing. Jesus had the ability to take a story and make it resonate in a deeply spiritual and profound manner. Although no one will ever duplicate the divine mastery of Jesus, still Jackson's place as a world-class storyteller is apparent—so much so, in fact, that he is now the highest paid director in Hollywood history.

Greg Wright has been carefully following the career of Jackson for some time now. He has conducted key interviews and is known for his critical reviews of Jackson's cinematic work. In this book he brings all those years of scholarship and intimate experience together. Greg has a way of reaching below the surface and bringing to light new areas of understanding that most of us would otherwise miss.

I have been deeply impressed by the insight Greg has furnished us in his previous work, *Tolkien in Perspective: Sifting the Gold from the Glitter*, and now he undertakes the task of placing Peter Jackson in a cohesive perspective.

David Bruce
Webmaster, HollywoodJesus.com
White City, Oregon, July 2004

Introduction

This book is for people who watch movies.

I also watch movies—a lot of them. But over the last five years, I have found myself thoroughly immersed in one particular cinematic spectacle, presented to us in three parts: Peter Jackson's *The Lord of the Rings*. David Bruce, webmaster at HollywoodJesus.com, anticipated the surge of interest that would accompany Jackson's films, and recruited me to begin pre-release coverage during the summer of 2000. With the release of the Special Extended Edition of *The Return of the King* in December of 2004, the roller coaster ride finally comes to an end.

While much of my *Rings*-related work in the last five years has focused on Tolkien's three-part novel, this volume collects my essays and lectures regarding Peter Jackson's filmed adaptation. As the years progressed, of course, more information became available in a wide variety of formats—DVD commentary tracks, interviews, Special Extended Editions and so on. But I make no attempt here to smooth over inconsistencies or seeming contradictions in my early reading of Jackson's films, nor have I attempted to "correct" my essays where I was "wrong." My goal has never been to be "right" about Jackson and Tolkien or to make myself look good in a self-congratulatory fashion—instead, I have placed a higher value on responsible, sober analysis in order to stimulate deeper and more serious thinking on the part of the moviegoing public. I invite the reader to engage my critical assessments and to feel wildly free to disagree. There's a good chance that I've badly missed the mark. I am, after all, very human.

Tearing Into Jackson's *Rings*

Now, there are a great number of ways in which to critically approach any given film, and many of them are equally valid. The particular approach that I have employed in my coverage of *The Lord of the Rings* for Hollywood Jesus probably warrants some explanation.

Because the story told in *The Lord of the Rings* is so complex, and because each of Peter Jackson's films is so dense, I elected from the start to interpret Jackson's films through a lens with which I was extremely familiar: J. R. R. Tolkien's books. Given that Tolkien remarked that "*The Lord of the Rings* is of course a fundamentally religious and Catholic work,"[1] interpreting Jackson's work through Tolkien's vision necessarily introduces the subject of Christian faith. (For me, of course, this is natural. I'm an ordained Christian pastor, and I write for a website called Hollywood Jesus.) At the same time, there's much more at work in Peter Jackson's version of *The Lord of the Rings* than Christian symbolism and allusion.

Consider sculpting. A sculptor's artistic vision becomes apparent not only through the portion of the stone that he actually uses but also through the portions he chooses to chip away. We're impressed with Mount Rushmore, in part, because we know the raw material with which Borglum started. In the same way, I believe that it's possible to get a handle on Jackson's vision for *The Lord of the Rings* by discussing not only what the director included in his movies but also what he left out. What's more, by analyzing Jackson's films with this in view, we may also glean a more general insight into the pivotal role that film plays in our culture.

To gain an appreciation of the value of this approach, let's examine one of the bits of Tolkien's original sculpture that Jackson chiseled away—that is, a bit that he snipped away and left on the cutting room floor: the chapter titled, "The Voice of Saruman." Only the extended edition of *The Return of the King* can erase from our minds the image with which we are left at the climax of *The Two Towers*, that of a perplexed and forlorn wizard surveying the flotsam and jetsam of Isengard. And while the longer versions of Jackson's films yield great insight into several of Tolkien's characters, Jackson still offers no satisfactory answer to the question: "Why does Saruman so easily fall prey to the power of the Ring?" After all, he never comes within miles of Isildur's bane, and many who have been in the same room with it—even carried it themselves—seem to fare much better than does Saruman.

One answer, of course, is supplied by the nature of the Ring itself. It has a will of its own, as Gandalf tells the story: the Ring is quite capable of looking out for Itself, and exerting Itself upon those who may be useful in Its cause. Proximity doesn't seem to be the operative variable in this power equation; the key is character. As Gandalf remarks, "I am what Saruman should have been."[2]

Another answer may be found by stepping outside Middle-earth. What, in our own world, wields the kind of power manifest in Middle-earth's Rings of Power? To what might we be drawn in the way that Saruman is drawn to the Ring?

The Power of Film

Film itself is a touchstone art for our culture, and not just as entertainment. Film is also polemic. Because great power is associated with film, those who know how to wield such power can turn it to other ends than mere entertainment. Probably the most famous example of this in the 20th century was Leni Riefenstahl, the German filmmaker who made for Adolph Hitler what were widely considered propaganda films. These included *Triumph of the Will*, which documented the Nazi rallies at Nuremburg, and *Olympia*, a film about the Nazi-staged Olympic games in Berlin in 1936. Interestingly, Riefenstahl died only recently—on September 9, 2003 at 101 years of age—and to the end of her life defended *Triumph*, saying, "I was only interested in how I could make a film that was not stupid like a crude propagandist newsreel, but more interesting. It reflects the truth as it was then, in 1934. It is a documentary, not propaganda."[3]

On the flip side of the coin, we might consider the films of Oliver Stone. Now, I personally like Stone's films—not because I agree with Stone and his politics, nor with his often paranoid conspiracy theories, but because we always know where Oliver Stone stands. He doesn't hide his agenda. He's willing to tell us what he believes, and he's brave enough to put it all right out in the open. And as we might recall, his film *JFK* provoked an enormous media firestorm, not dissimilar to the controversy provoked by early screenings of Gibson's *Passion*. This was because Stone tampered with history, both recreating the Zapruder film and restaging the assassination of JFK, through cinematic technique making it appear as if he were showing us the actual Zapruder film—which he wasn't. Now, we might ask ourselves—and Stone would be pretty pleased if we did—why to this day the public can't see the real Zapruder film. But I won't digress, because the politics of the assassination investigation are not my point. However, if one chooses to "meddle in the affairs of Wizards," as Stone did, so to speak, one will incur their wrath. And Stone did this deliberately because, as he put it, he wanted to propose "a countermyth to the myth of the Warren Commission."[4] Now, that's a fine statement to make, because we are all certainly free to consider the Warren Commission's report a myth—after all, which one of us has ever read it? Which one of us could afford the months necessary to track down and digest its volumes? And this gets at the polemic power of film since Stone's three-hour tour de force really does compete with the Warren Commission's report as an alternative myth, subjectively based on Jim Garrison's perception of historic events.

Entertainer and filmmaker Michael Moore explains why film is such a potent force for shaping ideas and perceptions. "All art," he says, and "every piece of journalism manipulates sequence and things. Just the fact that you edit, that certain things get taken out or put back in. ... We are not talking about objectivity. We're talking about a *style*."[5] And so, even though the public consumes his films as factual, objective and informative, Moore is able to somewhat coyly refer to any one of his movies as "a documentary told with a narrative style."[6] So the sequence in *Bowling for Columbine* in which Charlton Heston walks away from Michael Moore, for instance, is as much a cinematic recreation and fabrication as Oliver Stone's Zapruder film—or Tom Grunick's manufactured tears in *Broadcast News*. And the sequence shapes a new Heston myth to compete in the public's mind with Cecil B. DeMille's Moses/Heston myth.

Moore correctly asserts that our expectation of objectivity from documentaries is unrealistic, because every film does adopt a subjective point of view. And when we view a film, we are seeing ideas presented from that particular point of view, not another one. So when we walk into the theatre and see *The Return of the King*, we are—guess what?—seeing the story retold from one artist's point of view, one person's interpretation of the story of *The Lord of the Rings*: in this case, Peter Jackson's interpretation, which he worked out with his writers and crew.

The Audience Response

George Bernard Shaw, the British playwright and essayist, rather presciently foretold that the cinema would one day help to determine what the public would think, not only in terms of politics but also with regard to morality. "The cinema is going to form the mind of England," Shaw wrote. "The national conscience, the national ideals and tests of conduct, will be those of the film."[7] In essence he was correct, and not just about England. The films that we see and the way that we see them— especially if we consume them without reflection—have the ability to shape what we think about morality and our role in the world.

For fifty years, readers have found *The Lord of the Rings* compelling, and at the tail end of that half-century the raw power of Tolkien's tale has made the "leap into hyperspace" with an assist from film's power boost. And audiences are responding. Why? I received an e-mail that illustrates:

> My brother is a minister in the Reformed Church in America in Brooklyn, in one of the oldest churches, in fact, in New York City. My dad is a retired minister in the Reformed Church in America too. So is my brother's wife. My brother reads the Bible in study every day. (I don't. I read it, I study it, in spurts.) Yet both of us make the claim that *The Lord of the Rings* is our Scriptures. How? And why? Because it proclaims the truth of the Evangelium. If I am a Christian, if I remain a Christian, it probably has far more to do with the impression *The Lord of the Rings* made on my heart than any number of hours of Bible study or church attendance. And I suspect it's the same with many others, including those who, because they've only heard of Christianity as some sort of crude, abstract transactional bargain between various sides of God's supposed nature—his perfection and his justice, on the one hand, and his love on the other—would say they want nothing to do with it, and maybe embrace Wicca or something equally silly instead. And yet I've no doubt that they'd be People of Jesus, in spirit.[8]

Now, I don't necessarily endorse this writer's point of view, but his message does illustrate that Tolkien's creation—and Peter Jackson's presentation of it—warrants examination and close consideration. Socrates reportedly observed that the "unexamined life is not worth living." We might also say that the unexamined film is not worth viewing—further, that the unexamined film represents an abdication of living, and its attendant responsibilities.

Why? Because as the One Ring is Middle-earth's Weapon of Mass Destruction, film also represents the same kind of potent power. We might do well to reflect on the words of Saruman:

We must have power, power to order all things as we will, for that good which only the Wise can see. ... A new Power is rising. ... We may join with that Power. It would be wise, Gandalf. There is hope that way. ... The Wise, such as you and I, may with patience come at last to direct its courses, to control it. We can bide our time, we can keep our thoughts in our hearts, deploring maybe evils done by the way, but approving the high and ultimate purpose. ... There need not be, there would not be, any real change in our designs, only in our means. ... If we could command [the Ruling Ring], then the Power would pass to *us*.[9]

Like Saruman, we might think that power of any sort, whether it's the Ring or film, is something we may harness without coming under its control or influence. And we would be wrong. If we dare to approach the power of film, we would be wise to handle it with care and, like Gandalf or Aragorn, to be wary when we are in its presence. Yet we can also agree with Gandalf that there is "something else at work, beyond any design of the Ring-maker. ... And that may be an encouraging thought."[10]

A Critical Response

Some might also chafe at the idea of extensive dissection of a masterful work of art like Peter Jackson's *The Lord of the Rings*. Again, as Gandalf observes, "He that breaks a thing to find out what it is has left the path of wisdom."[11]

But perhaps the greatest danger in this whole enterprise is for the critic—for me, that is, as well as others—to think that, by delving into the depths of Jackson's vision and guiding others along with me, I am somehow doing a great good. Gandalf also cautioned, "The way of the Ring to my heart is by pity, pity for weakness and the desire of strength to do good. Do not tempt me! I dare not take it, not even to keep it safe, unused."[12]

If I would caution others to be cognizant of the potent power of film, I must also remind myself that the power of film over my own heart may very well be simply this: a temptation to turn that power toward my own private version of the greater good.

Ultimately, if we choose to meddle in the affairs of Wizards, or of filmmakers, we should remember the vain pride in Saruman's frustration that Wizards must "serve as counselors and helpers to stubborn, foolish beings who lack their store of wisdom and knowledge," as Brian Overland says.

> How tempting—when Gandalf could have so easily arranged it for him and Saruman to share the Ring—to just take the power and run everything for the greater good of Middle-earth? The attitude of Saruman is the perennial outlook of the man who must take over at all costs, because he is convinced that he knows better. That's what Saruman is selling: "I have to enslave you, for your own good. I may have to hurt or even kill you, for your own good." It is the dark side of Plato's philosopher king, who must establish his power by force. It is the perennial bill of goods sold by Machiavelli, Frederick Nietzsche, Marx, Lenin, fascism, and so many others.[13]

What bill of goods are we buying when we walk into a theatre? What bill of goods are we trying to sell by our dissection of film? It's a dangerous equation, to be sure. And like Federico Fellini, we might come to the conclusion, at the end of the day, that whether we make a film or view a film—and even if that film is "about a fillet of sole," Fellini says—"it would be about me."[14]

> *When we experience a film, we consciously prime ourselves for illusion. Putting aside will and intellect, we make way for it in our imagination.[15]*
>
> —Ingmar Bergman

Elements of this introductory essay were originally delivered as a lecture titled "Power and the Abuse of Power" in October 2003.

Notes

[1] J. R. R. Tolkien, Letters (Boston & New York: Houghton Mifflin Company, 2000), no. 142, to Robert Murray, 1953.

[2] J. R. R. Tolkien, The Two Towers 2nd ed. (Boston: Houghton Mifflin Company, 1965), p. 98.

[3] Leni Riefenstahl, quoted in "Film-maker Leni Riefenstahl dies." (BBC News, World Edition, 9 Sep. 2003). 2 July 2004 [http://news.bbc.co.uk/2/hi/entertainment/3093154.stm].

[4] Oliver Stone, Interview with Gavin Smith "The camera for me is an actor" (Film Comment January–February 1994) p. 39.

[5] Michael Moore, Interview with Harlan Jacobson "Michael and Me" (Film Comment November–December 1989) p. 23f.

[6] Ibid., p. 23.

[7] G. B. Shaw, in The Columbia World of Quotations (Columbia University Press, 1996 Online Edition Bartleby.com, 2001), Quote #53707. 2 July 2004 [www.bartleby.com].

[8] Henry P. Meeter [henry.meeter@t-online.de], "RE: Relationship to Lewis ..." (Private e-mail message to Greg Wright, [hjpastorgreg@hotmail.com] 5 September 2003).

[9] J. R. R. Tolkien, The Fellowship of the Ring 2nd ed. (Boston: Houghton Mifflin Company, 1965), p. 272f.

[10] Ibid., p. 65.

[11] Ibid., p. 272.

[12] Ibid., p. 71.

[13] Brian Overland [Briano2u@aol.com], "RE: October LOTR Feature at Hollywood Jesus." (Private e-mail message to Greg Wright, [hjpastorgreg@hotmail.com] 15 October 2003).

[14] Federico Fellini, in James B. Simpson, Simpson's Contemporary Quotations (Boston & New York: Houghton Mifflin and Company, 1988 Online Edition Bartleby.com, 2001), Quote #6221. 2 July 2004 [www.bartleby.com].

[15] Ingmar Bergman, in The Columbia World of Quotations (Columbia University Press, 1996 Online Edition Bartleby.com, 2001), Quote #6829. 2 July 2004 [www.bartleby.com].

From Book to Screen

LECTURE, DECEMBER 2003

❧ Doing Justice to *The Lord of the Rings* ❧

The differences between the art form of the novel and the medium of film are not widely understood or appreciated. Audiences demand different things from their books than they demand from their movies—and yet, when a popular work like *The Lord of the Rings* is translated to celluloid, audiences seem to want to have their cake and eat it, too. Can J. R. R. Tolkien's story work as a film while losing nothing of the novel's inspired vision?

The obstacles to reducing over 500,000 words to three filmable screenplays were not insignificant. Deciding which scenes to cut and which to alter or add must have been agonizing—and the need to involve the enormous fan-base only exacerbated the pain. The elements that survived the trimming—and those that didn't—tell us a great deal about the filmmakers and about the audience.

While ultimately a film is an entirely different beast from a book, and can't be expected to deliver the same sort of impact, Peter Jackson and key screenwriters Philippa Boyens and Fran Walsh did endeavor to keep their work consistent with "the spirit" of Tolkien's magnum opus. But what does that mean, precisely?

My experience and background with *The Lord of the Rings*

13

goes back to my high school years, when I first read the trilogy at my brother's suggestion. I was also assigned Tolkien's books to read in both high school and college, where I first started dealing critically with *The Lord of the Rings*. For the last several years now, I've been covering the release of the movies for HollywoodJesus.com, writing a series of monthly articles and being an online information resource—dealing with fan mail and questions regarding the movies and books.

One reason I'm intrigued by the process of adapting the novel into films is that, over the last several years, I've heard from a host of people who don't appreciate the difficulty of that process. And it's very easy, if one is a fan of the books, to watch the movies and feel that Peter Jackson has done a horrible job of adapting Tolkien's literally fantastic story. But it isn't an easy task, and there are a number of issues involved worth discussing.

Many critics—and yes, I'm one of them—also write things about the movies, and about Tolkien, that may seem very strange to the average person. Critics often fancy themselves experts; sometimes they are, sometimes they aren't. But often they simply communicate what they know in a way that is impenetrable or irrelevant to an entertainment-seeking audience.

So before we address Jackson's attempt to capture the spirit of Tolkien, a good place to begin is with a discussion of the similarities and differences between novels and films.

❧ Narrative Structure ❧

Novels and movies all share a common narrative structure, first described thousands of years ago by Aristotle and characterized by certain components. The first of these basic components is the pairing of the story's protagonist and antagonist, or what we commonly refer to as the hero and the villain. The conflict between the two drives the story and brings it to a resolution, doing so in a fairly standard and consistent way, regardless of the mode or length of the story.

The narrative components that Aristotle described were formalized in the 19th century by novelist and playwright Gustav Freytag. High school or college literature students may be familiar with the so-called "Freytag's Triangle" (Figure 1).

The first part of the story, called "exposition," sets up the basic elements of the storyline and lays out a number of details that establish character relationships and the setting of the story. As the plot starts to develop, this introductory material gives us some idea of where the story is headed.

Then we move into the "inciting" of the plot, or the conflict between protagonist and antagonist—the rising action of the story. This is where most tales spend the lion's share of their time—building the tension, working out character relationships, developing the conflict between the heroes and villains (maybe even clarifying who the heroes and villains really are). The action builds steadily, culminating in the climax or "central crisis": the apex of Freytag's Triangle.

Following the climax is the section of the story called the "denouement," or the wrapping-up. Now, we might ask: Why doesn't the story just end at the climax? Why doesn't the story end right at its peak?

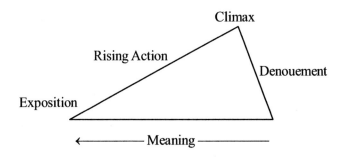

Figure 1: Freytag's Triangle

Aristotle argued that every story needs a denouement in order to tie the ending of the story back to its beginning—thereby forming the base of Freytag's Triangle and giving the story some satisfying meaning. The denouement resolves the conflict and tidies up the plot's loose ends. Without its base, the Triangle collapses.

This basic narrative structure generally works for any story that's told. Detailed studies of story structure reveal, interestingly enough, that even very unusual or avant-garde storytelling almost always comes back to this ancient and basic model.

In a novel, however, the writer has the luxury of departing from this structure to a degree. Due to the flexibility of a novel's length, a writer can actually extend the denouement (Figure 2), making the falling action of the story less precipitous. In this way, a larger portion of the story may be used to resolve details of the plot—sometimes necessary in a novel. If the plot is sufficiently complex, or there are a great number of characters involved, the writer may also need to spend more time tying up loose ends, so that the reader doesn't feel as though issues have been left unaddressed. As we know, stories often raise numerous questions that readers insist on having answered.

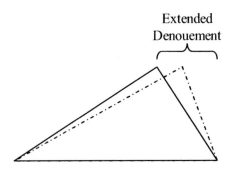

Extended
Denouement

Figure 2: The Novel's Structure

In a film, the structure typically differs somewhat, and looks more like what we'd find in a short story rather than in a novel. In the typical film, the denouement tends to be noticeably truncated (Figure 3), and for good reason. Generally speaking, films are based on short-story structures rather than on the structure of novels. In a short story, there are fewer characters, and fewer plot details to wrap up. In fact, a short story tends to drive toward a specific climax, and the conflict is usually resolved very close to the end of the story. This results in very steep falling action to conclude the narrative. If we reflect on most movies that we see, we may easily observe this short-story characteristic: like its literary cousin, a film also tends to build toward a climax very close to its end, and perhaps only the last five to seven minutes of running time are spent wrapping things up.

❧ The Structure of *The Lord of the Rings* ☙

At this point, the direction of this discussion may become readily apparent since many films, and especially Peter Jackson's adaptations of *The Lord of the Rings,* don't completely conform to the standard short-story structure. They spend a little more time

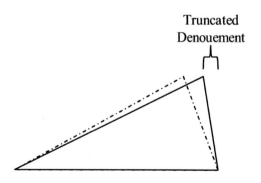

Figure 3: The Film's Structure

than is typical wrapping things up at the end, again for good reasons. One is the fact that Jackson's films are longer than average—and the longer the film, the greater percentage of running time that can be allocated to the denouement. But a weightier reason is that there are some very complex factors in breaking down Tolkien's 500,000-word novel into three distinct movies.

First, Jackson is breaking up a single story into three parts (Figure 4). This is no mean feat, considering that the original story's structure conforms, generally speaking, to Freytag's Triangle. If a single story structure were to be neatly chopped into three pieces, what would happen? The first segment would tend to be heavy on exposition, with no real climax and no wrap-up whatsoever. If we took Tolkien's *The Fellowship of the Ring* and filmed it exactly as written, we wouldn't have a very satisfying climax. In a second segment based solely on what Tolkien wrote in *The Two Towers*, we would really be in a bind because we would have no beginning to our story and virtually no ending either. That's a big problem. And the running time of the third segment, *The Return of the King*, would primarily be occupied with the story's climax and a disproportionate denouement.

This leads us to the second major complication in breaking

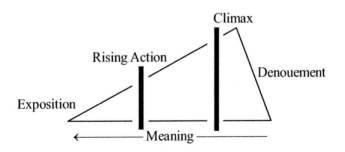

Figure 4: Breaking Up Tolkien's Story

down Tolkien's novel, because the author himself defies the conventions of narrative structure. In *The Lord of the Rings*, Tolkien takes over one hundred and fifty pages just to wrap up his story—and this protracted denouement itself incorporates a complete, self-contained triangular narrative structure (Figure 5). Even films with extended running times are not capable of supporting rising action within the denouement.

Narrative difficulties aside, the director and screenwriters confronted a third major obstacle to their adaptation: the novel's enormous fan base. There are a host of people who love *The Lord of the Rings* and have their own ideas about how the story should be presented on film: who their favorite characters are, what their favorite scenes are, even how they would adapt the story if they were given the opportunity to do so.

Back in 1978, a director named Ralph Bakshi attempted to film *The Lord of the Rings* as an animated feature, and he adapted it in two parts rather than three. He broke the story smack in the middle, right after the battle at Helm's Deep—essentially the point at which Peter Jackson's *The Two Towers* ends. Because Bakshi's film was such a commercial disaster that he failed to secure financing for the sequel, his version literally tells only half of the story and has no real ending at all.

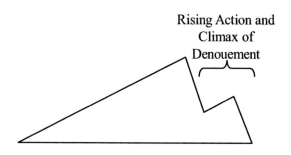

Rising Action and
Climax of
Denouement

Figure 5: Structure of *The Lord of the Rings*

The second half of that story ended up being told in an animated feature produced by Rankin/Bass—the same outfit that also animated *The Hobbit* for television. Over the years, untold numbers of kids have seen this version of *The Return of the King*, which features the famous refrain, "Frodo of the Nine Fingers…"[1] And that film also wasn't very satisfying, of course, because it also told only half of the story, utilizing a flashback story structure with very little exposition or rising tension.

So Peter Jackson tackled a very difficult and unprecedented task in attempting to tell the entire story over the course of three films. Since I am a fan of *The Lord of the Rings* and a critic as well, I have, of course, raised my own particular objections to Peter Jackson's adaptation. But over all, he has managed to do a pretty decent job.

We can discover how he managed this remarkable feat by first going back to *The Lord of the Rings* and examining what it is that makes Tolkien's novel work.

༄ How Tolkien's Novel Works ༅

The core of *The Lord of the Rings* is simply a terrific story about Bilbo's Ring being taken from the Shire through incredibly difficult circumstances and trials to Mount Doom to be destroyed. How the Ring gets there—and for the reader, wondering if the Ring will, in fact, get there—is the primary source of narrative tension: finding out who the villains and the heroes of the story really are. The story told in *The Lord of the Rings* is tremendously interesting, wondrous and engrossing.

It is also built on very interesting characters. The Elves in the story are a very unusual people, because they don't seem to be like any Elves we may have read about in other stories. But Tolkien didn't invent the Elves. They were at least based on something else with which he was familiar.

At the center of the story, however, are the Hobbits, an entirely new creation with Tolkien—and they are what makes the story really work. They are what made fans ask for a sequel to *The Hobbit*, giving Tolkien a reason to find another Hobbit story that he wanted to tell. And what are Hobbits, besides short and furry-footed? They are, according to Tolkien, "a branch of the specifically human race."[2] So even though they aren't like men in all respects, they share, as far as Tolkien is concerned, a great deal of human history. They come from the same source, and are very much like men, having both a body and a spirit. The differences intrigue us, and the similarities draw us in.

In addition to his characters, Tolkien incorporated into his story what literature teachers call "archetypes"—what in film language we might call "stock characters." While "serious" literature frequently makes use of archetypes, "serious" films rarely indulge in stock characters. Steven Spielberg, for instance, while a master of film shorthand and entertaining utilization of stock characters (think *Always* or *Hook*), has only won wide critical acclaim for the films in which he has opted for protracted character development (such as *Amistad*, *Schindler's List* and *Saving Private Ryan*). This is perhaps counterintuitive since a film's limited running time works against portrayal of "realistic" characters. This also complicates the job of adapting *The Lord of the Rings* since in Tolkien's novel there are not many characters that really have what we might call "three dimensions." A short digression will illustrate the point.

Faramir is, in essence, a stock character in Tolkien's novel— a heroic stock character, but a stock character nonetheless. Recalling the Aristotelian model of story structure, we may observe that a story's principal characters all have an "arc" that parallels the rising action, climax and denouement of the story itself. The characters develop and change as the story progresses. That's not really the case, though, for an archetypal character: one who is fully defined going into the story, helping shape the action and plot but not being transformed or significantly shaped by them. So in *The Lord of the Rings*, the novel, we find in Faramir a man who is principled, who doesn't have to battle with his will to resist the temptation of the Ring. He seems to possess the strength of character to resist the temptation of the Ring, and doesn't have to learn how to do that. Later, during the denouement, Faramir does have to learn how to love and how to become a healer; but during the rising action of the story he serves as a contrast to his brother Boromir, who very much does have a problem with the Ring, who does have a problem with temptation to power—and who, because he is more "realistic" in this sense, has the power to move and shape the rising action of the plot.

In Jackson's movies, however, there is little contrast between Faramir and Boromir. They both act on the same motivation: a desire to please their father. They both attempt to bring the Ring back to Gondor. And this parallel between *The Fellowship of the Ring* and *The Two Towers* works in Jackson's favor. So why is Tolkien interested in putting archetypes into his story in the first place, if they're not necessary in the films?

Tolkien was more of a classicist. He was interested in—and based his own work on—classic models of literature. He studied works such as *Beowulf* and was raised on Arthurian legend and classic volumes of fairy tales. And medieval literature doesn't tend to be filled with three-dimensional characters; in fact, quite the opposite. It tends to be filled with archetypes—characters that don't necessarily learn anything at all. They begin the story fully realized, and because of their identity and qualities they themselves drive the action rather than being shaped by the action. They are frequently tragic, flawed characters rather than dramatic, dynamic characters.

Archetypes allow readers a familiar and comfortable point of view, a moral or narrative reference point from which the story can be processed. This was extremely important to the fundamental design of *The Lord of the Rings* as it was written, particularly given the scope and length of the story. Tolkien's written tale would be difficult to digest otherwise.

Another technique that Tolkien employs in *The Lord of the*

Rings is the use of symbols: elements that put meaning into the story in ways that might or might not register consciously in the reader's mind. As an example of Tolkien's symbols, we need look no further than the Ring itself. I wear a ring myself that physically appears very much like the One Ring—but my ring doesn't have the same weight, either literally or figuratively, as does the Ring in Tolkien's story.

In *The Lord of the Rings*, the Ring is more than just a band of gold. It represents Power, and whatever might lead us astray in our lives—whatever might cause us, like Boromir, to betray the Fellowship, so to speak. For some people it might be political power; for others it might be social influence or control issues; for still others it might even be something as familiar as alcohol. But we all have powers in our lives to which we are vulnerable, and in accompanying Frodo on his journey to Mount Doom we each symbolically carry our own Ring to the same destruction. The Ring becomes a central symbol, deliberately crafted by Tolkien.

A wealth of symbols fills Tolkien's story, and we won't take the time to delve into them all. But it is important to understand the role of symbols—which allow the readers to identify, either consciously or unconsciously, with the action or crisis of the story—and to understand that those symbols serve as essential elements of the story's power. They are there intentionally. They are part of what makes *The Lord of the Rings* successful as a novel.

❧ How Jackson's Films Work ❧

So what makes *The Lord of the Rings* work on film? This is a relevant question because many of the elements that made Tolkien's story work as a novel get broken down or lost when the novel is turned into a film.

The first decision that Jackson and his writers made—and it was a very sound choice—was to transform Tolkien's epic tale into three distinct stories. They didn't just break *The Lord of the*

Rings up into a single screenplay and say, "Let's tell Part One of the story first, then Part Two, and then Part Three." Instead, they restructured the novel in very significant ways, making each one of the three films work more or less as a standalone story. Again, if we recall Freytag's Triangle, we will realize, as Jackson did, that *The Fellowship of the Ring* would need to have its own climax and denouement; that *The Two Towers* would need to have its own beginning as a story, as well as its own climax and denouement; and that for *The Return of the King*, the writers would have to work diligently to craft an opening sequence that plays like the legitimate beginning of a film. With these objectives having been accomplished, each section of the original story then becomes, to a degree, its own self-contained, complete story. And Jackson accomplished those objectives fairly successfully.

The second reason that Jackson's films are successful, as films, is the fact that they *are* films—and films have three primary artistic components to them while a novel has just one. A novel comprises words on a printed page, and (as Sean Astin observes based on his own studies) the reader and author interact in the reader's mind through those words to create the world of the story.[3] But a film is more complex than that. Film is an art form than employs not only words, but pictures—at 24 frames each second—and music, too. The combination of these three components (each of which is tremendously powerful by itself) produces art that has the capacity, when well executed, to be more powerful than any one of these components individually.

Is a film always as powerful as a book? No. But the potential is there. And Peter Jackson utilizes that potential very wisely in each one of his movies, making each quite satisfying as a standalone film.

To illustrate the measure of Jackson's success in this regard, we really need only compare *The Two Towers* with the second installment of the original Star Wars series, *The Empire Strikes Back*. While there are elements of that film which are admirable (and in many ways superior to George Lucas' first entry in the series), the film ultimately doesn't work very well. Though it has a satisfying climax, it has no proper ending. It's literally a cliffhanger, with plenty of unfinished business—and Han Solo left frozen in a block of carbon. There's almost a tag on the end that says, "To be continued." Properly speaking, it's all rising action and no denouement.

But Jackson avoided that trap with *The Two Towers*. His writers restructured the larger story so that each film is self-contained enough to work fairly well on its own merits. This is accomplished by creatively building tension, by rearranging story elements and bringing in new ones (as much as we might chafe at the idea). The romance in each of the first two films, for instance, is amplified well beyond what Tolkien included in his novel. Purists will know that Arwen appears only by reference in *The Fellowship of the Ring*; in the movie, however, she is the one who brings Frodo to Rivendell on horseback, and she's also the one who stops the Black Riders at the river. It's even hinted in the first movie that she might show up in battle later on, as Jackson originally planned.

Why was that necessary? Because the filmmakers knew that movie audiences respond to romance, even require it. And while there's not romance as we might think of it in other movies—something as overt as *Aladdin* or as steamy as *Troy*—there is romance nonetheless, and audiences have responded to it. And in *The Two Towers*, the thwarted romance between Éowyn and Aragorn is amplified and escalated by the introduction of "dream" sequences with Aragorn's true love, Arwen. Both threads then come together in *The Return of the King*—and romance has become a significant factor in all three films.

Jackson's writers also developed a distinct hero and villain in each of the movies. Tolkien's story really has just one hero and one villain. While we may argue about who the "real" hero of the story is, we will likely agree that Sauron (and the embodiment of his power in the Ring itself) fills the villain's role in the novel. But what about in the films?

❧ Peter Jackson's Three Films ❧

In Jackson's *Fellowship*, the primary tension arises within the Fellowship itself. The conflict in the movie is: what is going to happen to the Fellowship? Will it survive? Are they going to stick together and manage to fulfill their quest? The hero of this section of the story, of course, is Frodo, not only in his faithful relationship with Sam but also in his selfless acceptance of a seemingly impossible task. The climax of the story, in fact, is Frodo and Sam's resolve to carry through where the Fellowship has failed; the story ultimately becomes not about succeeding, but about perseverance. Success or failure as we tend think of them become irrelevant. And the villain that is working against this resolve is the Ring itself. It draws evil to the Fellowship in the Shire, at Caradhras, in Moria and even in Lórien. The Ring drives conflict throughout the story—even driving wedges between Gandalf, Bilbo and Frodo—and instigates the climax of the story: Boromir's attempt to take the Ring (and subsequent heroic death) and Frodo's subsequent resolve to go on alone. *Fellowship* has its own viable characters, tension, romance, heroes and villains.

Though perhaps more difficult to discern, the internal tension of *The Two Towers* is also well-crafted, and this is no mean feat for Jackson. As the middle of the three films, *Towers* has the least defined section of the overarching story, and is also the darkest episode, devoid of either the glowing light of the Shire or the thrill of final deliverance.

To overcome these obstacles and create a successful story, the filmmakers turned Saruman into the principal villain, and so successfully that we may easily miss the fact that the Ring itself plays a relatively small role in this episode. Since the Fellowship is divided, the Ring can't drive the action in both halves of the story. Frodo is headed toward Mordor with the Ring, and the rest of the Fellowship is going the opposite direction toward Rohan and Isengard. And even though the Ring and its effect are still responsible for these events, it's not visibly present as it was in

Fellowship, hanging on the chain, clutched continually by Frodo and tempting the entire Fellowship. The visual villainy, instead, is provided by the titular towers themselves and the treachery that Saruman orchestrates from Orthanc. The tension between the two towers—how Saruman will end up being a factor in the War of the Ring—comes to a head at the climactic battle at Helm's Deep, where Saruman's army is destroyed; and in the denouement, we see Isengard being swept clean by a massive flood. Saruman is impotently stranded in the tower with Wormtongue at his side: conflict resolved, villain defeated. From a cinematic standpoint, Saruman even becomes a nonissue in *The Return of the King*.

And who's the hero of *The Two Towers*? Aragorn, who becomes literally heroic as the story progresses. In a subtle conclusion to *The Fellowship of the Ring*, Aragorn prepares to pursue the Orcs with Legolas and Gimli—and dons Boromir's greaves, taking up the figurative gauntlet and accepting the mantle of leadership. To start with, Peter Jackson's Aragorn is not at all confident of who he is and what he is meant to be. Jackson provides him with plentiful disappointments: Elrond discouraging his pursuit of Arwen, constant reminders that the power of Men has faded, and a general disregard for his counsel. By the conclusion of *Towers*, though, he's the only leader capable of taking charge at Helm's Deep. And he is widely acknowledged as the hero of the battle.

The Two Towers works surprisingly well as a film. Initially, I was skeptical of its success. I did not think it would be as popular as *The Fellowship of the Ring*, but it has actually out-grossed *Fellowship*, both in the United States and around the world.

Despite box office results, however, *The Return of the King* is possibly the least satisfactory of the three films—from the standpoint of pure storytelling. Jackson and his writers do manage to invent an amazingly effective opening sequence that manages to introduce a traditional Aristotelian story structure. And from there, tension builds nicely toward the true climax of Tolkien's story at Mount Doom. But then Jackson replicates, after his own fashion, the same unconventional rule-breaking choice made by Tolkien: a protracted denouement.

What is the effect? In a conventional movie ending, the final five to seven minutes of denouement leave the audience riding the emotional high of the story's climax. *The Return of the King*, however, affects audiences differently because the denouement falls away very, very gradually. When audiences leave *The Return of the King*, they are more frequently reflecting on the implications of the story and its meaning than they are riding an emotional high. Think about it: *The Return of the King* is not *The Return of the Jedi*.

For many audiences (and particularly critics), however, Jackson's multiple endings merely detract from the story's climax. Oddly enough, history may demonstrate that *The Return of the King*, though technically not the most efficiently or effectively told story of the three, will prove to be the most resonant. Box office figures and *The Return of the King*'s eleven Academy Awards certainly point in that direction.

❧ The Cutting Room Floor ❧

What did Peter Jackson cut out? Because Jackson's movies have been successful, the answer to this question is particularly instructive. Though some fans have obviously objected to deviations from Tolkien's books, Jackson and his writers have just as obviously made no catastrophic errors (though their original intentions with Arwen came close). Not every element of Tolkien's design could be retained, of course. But which elements did Jackson ultimately deem dispensable?

Probably the most significant cut is the sequence in the Old Forest and Barrow Downs with Tom Bombadil. Anyone who has read the novel remembers that episode, if without understanding it. Most readers think: Who is Tom Bombadil? What the heck is he? He's not an Elf. He's not a Man. He's not an Ent; he's not a Wizard. He's not a Hobbit. What is he?

Tolkien's story doesn't define what Bombadil is. And if we're telling the story, particularly on film, Bombadil may be a convenient element to omit. How do we answer those questions? How do we wrap up a loose end like that? Tolkien himself never does. He breaks one of the standard storytelling rules by throwing in a sequence in the middle of his story that doesn't "advance the plot," that doesn't answer any questions. It only raises questions. Naturally, Jackson and company simply decided not to deal with Bombadil.

Interestingly, the extended edition of *The Two Towers* puts some of Tom Bombadil's lines in the mouth of Treebeard. There's even a tree in Fangorn, similar to Old Man Willow in Tolkien's book, from which Treebeard must rescue Merry and Pippin. The filmmakers recognized that there are some important implications to Tom Bombadil and they didn't want to eliminate him entirely, but they also couldn't spend twenty minutes of a movie explaining Bombadil and making him work as a character. So Old Tom? Sorry. He gets the axe.

To me, one of the most significant cuts in the movies—and this is spoken both as a fan and as a critic—is the effort that Tolkien put into creating a sensible flow of time and space. Jackson's version simply does not do justice to Tolkien's detailed geography and plot orchestration. Readers who are so inclined may examine Tolkien's maps to form an adequate understanding of where the characters are and how they move from place to place. The more attentive among us may even note that if the moon is rising in one thread of the story it is also rising in another concurrent thread of the story. Tolkien pays close attention to distances, the time it takes for people to travel from one location to another, and how all the various geographic and temporal dimensions coalesce at the end of the story. The movies, however, make little attempt to preserve Tolkien's orderly progression of events.

We should expect, however, that Jackson's bag of tricks is quite different from Tolkien's. In *The Fellowship of the Ring*,

Jackson makes great use of the common cinematic technique of collapsing time and space. Even the simplest program on TV may feature a scene in which a character comes through a door and then crosses the room—and we very rarely actually see the character physically walk across the entire room. Instead, the director will show a clip of the character walking through the door, perhaps coming toward the camera, then cut to another character's reaction in a different part of the room. When the film cuts back, the first character has now completed the trip across the room. The viewer's mind fills in the blanks, naturally assuming, without actually having seen it happen, that the person has simply crossed the room—and without noticing that insufficient time has elapsed for the person to have actually covered that distance.

In *Fellowship*, this technique is used to great advantage. By cutting back and forth between various elements of the storyline, Jackson can make days at a time disappear—even weeks—without disorienting viewers in the least. So while the Hobbits clearly spend several weeks traveling from the Shire to Rivendell, the Fellowship appears to take roughly the same amount of time journeying from Rivendell to Parth Galen, where Boromir dies. The book, however, makes it abundantly clear that a month elapses between Rivendell and Lorien, and another month between Lorien and Parth Galen. For Tolkien, the passage of time is consistent and proportional to the distance traveled. In Jackson's *Fellowship*, however, the audience might easily get the impression that only a few days, rather than weeks, pass between the loss of Gandalf in Moria and Boromir's death—and for the most part, it doesn't really matter. The technique works, though it may annoy purists. The medium of film simply doesn't require the same kind of consistency of time and space that a book demands.

In *The Two Towers*, time and space are condensed even further. Watching the theatrical release, I found myself thinking, "Where on earth did Merry and Pippin go?" They vanish from the narrative for three or four days, and we have no idea what they have been up to—and the characters themselves don't seem to know either. When we leave them, they're traveling through Fangorn with Treebeard, and when we rejoin them, they're still riding around with the Ent. There's no sign whatsoever that they've exchanged any substantial information with him. They don't appear to have done anything either. What have they been doing? But in the book, we know exactly what's happened during that entire sequence and can account, day by day, for how the Hobbits have spent their time. The extended edition of *Towers* restores much of that detail, and in a very entertaining fashion.

The Return of the King furthers the temporal distortions, drawing out Frodo's trek through the Morgul Vale to Cirith Ungol over several days—and all the while Théoden and Aragorn separately cover impossible distances, Aragorn on foot and Théoden on horseback. Even more disconcerting, the journey of the Captains of the West from Minas Tirith to the Black Gate occupies less than an afternoon of Frodo and Sam's story. But all these changes merely demonstrate how cinematic compression techniques make such sleight of hand nearly imperceptible.

Plot points and minor characters are not the only casualties in Jackson's films, however. As noted above, many of Tolkien's archetypes are also sacrificed—and one of the key victims is Aragorn. When he first encounters the Hobbits at Bree, they have no idea who this Ranger is. Well, who is he indeed? The movie gives very little explanation, in part because Jackson's Aragorn himself is not really sure. In the book, however, the Hobbits find out the first time they encounter Aragorn who he is: they have a delayed note from Gandalf, attesting to Aragorn's identity. He has his own prophetic rhyme, and carries the shards of Narsil: "the crownless again shall be king."[4] And, of course, Aragorn himself knows, from the very time we meet him, that he is the heir of Isildur, that he's the rightful King of Gondor. In stark contrast, Jackson's Aragorn doesn't want to be king. According to Elrond, he has chosen exile instead. Aragorn is entirely unsure of himself and his future.

Jackson elects to present a different Aragorn from the one in the books because, as an archetype, Aragorn is a man who was born to be king. The moment his mother names him, he is the fulfillment of prophecy. Everybody close to him knows his identity and what he is destined to become. Arwen knows. Elrond knows. Gandalf knows. And over the years, Aragorn serves in the armies of Gondor and Rohan under an assumed identity, careful not to prematurely reveal himself to the enemy. He's not hiding out in the wilderness; at Gandalf's bidding, he and the other Dúnedain are protecting the Shire from dark forces that would otherwise destroy it. He is royalty with a very low profile, and he knows that he is going to be crowned king. When and how only remain to be seen. In Peter Jackson's adaptation, however, Aragorn must be convinced to become a king.

Is Jackson's portrayal of Aragorn fatal to the movies? Does the loss of key archetypes make the movies fail? Not at all. But archetypes are one of the major casualties in making the transition from the printed page to the silver screen—and this has everything to do with the needs of the audience.

ഗ **The Role of the Audience** ബ

Movies tend to focus on different issues from books. And if Jackson's movies are, in part, about Aragorn learning to accept his role in the world, what advantage is there in that? For one thing, an audience can more easily identify with such a hero. Who among us, after all, was born to be a king? Which of us knew, from the moment of birth, that the Presidency of the United States was simply in the cards: that's it, I'm the prophesied one, end of story? No, that just doesn't happen. Most of us are like Jackson's Aragorn. We may have the capacity to be heroic, but we are going to need others to goad us into heroism. Circumstances are going to have transform us from "regular joes" into heroes—circumstances and, perhaps, what we choose to believe. And it simply may be tougher to believe in heroism today than it was in

1954. The needs of the audience have changed.

And the audience (as well as the critics) has a certain economic clout, the right to demand satisfaction for its entertainment dollar. If we don't like what we see, we don't buy tickets. Perhaps we're lucky, though, that Jackson was not saddled with that fiscal reality for *The Return of the King*. The first two movies were so successful that the studio let Peter Jackson do with the third what he wanted. And he has proven to have fine instincts. He is a good director, and he works with excellent writers. He knows what he likes, and what he likes works for audiences.

What he likes also happens to be very close to the heart of Tolkien's tale. The story of *The Lord of the Rings* is about the value of the simple life. Its heart is in the Hobbits, Hobbiton and the Shire. A simpler time and a simpler life: good, humble, basic pleasures to which we long to return at the end of a war.

The Lord of the Rings is about evil in the world and technological "progress," and the danger that technology represents—and, yes, the temptation into which such dangerous power may lead. And yet there are also other powers in the world.

As Peter Jackson's Gandalf tells Frodo in the Mines of Moria, "All we have to decide is what to do with the time that is given to us. There are other forces at work in this world, Frodo, besides the will of evil. Bilbo was meant to find the Ring, in which case you also were meant to have it. And that is an encouraging thought."[5]

Tolkien's very theory of fantasy is built on such an encouraging thought: what Tolkien called "eucatastrophe," a word we won't find in the dictionary. It is a word Tolkien coined for the joy of the unlooked-for happy ending, a joy that catches a glimpse of the Biblical resurrection story—the triumph of God over sin, death and the grave. By paying homage to the "eucatastrophe of the story of the Incarnation," Tolkien says, the artist's "desire and aspiration of sub-creation has been raised to the fulfillment of Creation."[6] Eucatastrophe doesn't noisily preach the biblical story. Instead, the happy ending evokes the essence of the "good news." We like happy endings, Tolkien says, because we can't help being drawn to them.

If nothing else, the brutality of Mel Gibson's *The Passion of the Christ* demonstrates that the original eucatastrophic happy ending was not cheaply bought. Is *The Lord of the Rings* in part a dark story? Yes. Is *The Two Towers*, in particular, a very oppressive movie? Certainly. Are the battle sequences in *The Return of the King* heart-rendingly grim? Without a doubt. But why? Tolkien said that the threat of darkness—what he called "dyscatastrophe," anguish in the world—is necessary to the "joy of deliverance."[7]

It's an odd concept, perhaps, but one that survives the translation from book to screen—whether or not Jackson was aware of the theory. And where *Passion* perhaps offers only a glimpse of the joy of deliverance, Jackson's *The Lord of the Rings* serves it up in abundance.

Section Notes

[1] Glen Yarborough in The Return of the King Dir. Arthur Rankin, Jr. and Jules Bass, Perf. Orson Bean, John Huston Rankin/Bass Productions 1980 DVD (Warner Home Video, 2001).

[2] J. R. R. Tolkien, Letters (Boston & New York: Houghton Mifflin Company, 2000), footnote to no. 131, to Milton Waldman, 1951.

[3] Sean Astin, Interview with Greg Wright et al. "The Hobbit Next Door" (Hollywood Jesus 15 June 2004). 15 July 2004 [http://www.hollywoodjesus.com/lord_of_the_rings_interview_06.htm].

[4] J. R. R. Tolkien, The Fellowship of the Ring 2nd ed. (Boston: Houghton Mifflin Company, 1965), p. 182.

[5] Ian McKellen in The Fellowship of the Ring Dir. Peter Jackson, Perf. Ian McKellen, Elijah Wood, Viggo Mortensen New Line Cinema 2001 DVD (New Line Home Video 2002).

[6] J. R. R. Tolkien, The Tolkien Reader (New York: Ballantine Books, 1966), p. 88f.

[7] Ibid., p. 86.

Competing Visions

❧ Peter Jackson versus Ralph Bakshi ☙

AUGUST 2002

The Blessing...

1978 was a most excellent year in Seattle. The Seahawks, new to the NFL in 1976, were one of the most exciting teams in football, the Sonics were well on the way to becoming a championship caliber team under the coaching of Lenny Wilkens, I was entering my final year of high school, and I had fully immersed myself in Middle-earth. I think it's safe to say that by the time I was 14 or 15 I was a bona fide Tolkien fanatic. It still being the pre-Internet years, I was definitely not as well-informed as the average fan is today; in fact, even while in college at the University of Washington from 1979–1984, I don't think I ran into anyone who was more "into" Tolkien than I was. And I was an English Literature *and* Computer Science major! But by today's standards, my fandom was pretty infantile.

Still, the announcement that my final year of adolescence would be graced by the release of an animated treatment of *The Lord of the Rings* was almost more than I could bear. Earlier the previous year, I had finished the months-long, literally "painstaking" process of hand-copying enlarged versions of Tolkien's maps onto parchment, using remorselessly unforgiving India ink.

37

If learning to deal with a young male's hormones hadn't already been enough stress in my life, I'm sure that working on those maps *would* have sent me over the edge. And the prospect of seeing the geography of Middle-earth, now so well fixed in my head, on the big screen of Seattle's theatres was thrilling.

I was a bit perplexed, however, to learn that the animation was being directed by Ralph Bakshi. I had seen *Fritz the Cat* emblazoned on the marquee at the 3000-seat Lewis and Clark Theatre some years before; and I remembered that it was one of those controversial X-rated movies. Why wasn't Disney handling something as important as the artistic representation of Middle-earth? For years, the Hildebrandts had already been publishing artwork that would be a tough act to follow. Did United Artists think that the story needed a little more spice than brought to the table by the Hildebrandts' chivalric ladies? Were Bakshi's Goldberry and Galadriel going to be buck nekkid? Intriguing as the thought might have been to a teenage male, there were still, at this point in my life, some things that were sacred. And *The Lord of the Rings* was one of them. Nobody had better tamper with the chaste virtue of Tolkien's women!

So it was with some trepidation that I ventured to the theatre. There was enough advance word, though (through conventional press coverage), to inform me and other Tolkien fans that Bakshi's team had indeed taken some liberties with the storyline, and contrary to the historical revisionism of some latter-day critics, it was well known that this 140-minute-or-so film would cover only half of Tolkien's three-volume novel. My mind was open. It was not disappointed. The movie was serious, dark and violent. And I was aware that I was watching an art form—film animation—that I really didn't understand. Bakshi's use of "rotoscoping," somewhat new at the time, was very startling and (at times) extremely satisfying. Sequences such as the Prancing Pony at Bree left me feeling that Bakshi had really gotten a handle on how to film Tolkien, since live-action cinematography simply wasn't yet an option.

38

There was so much to enjoy about the film, in fact, that I saw it more than once, dragging friends with me on later visits. I particularly enjoyed the thrilling mayhem of Moria and Helm's Deep. I hunted for the soundtrack album, without success. I bought the 1979 Tolkien calendar featuring artwork from the movie (only marginally disappointed that Ballantine had failed to publish a Hildebrandt calendar that year). I bought copies of the movie posters (both versions) and placed them with pride on my walls, alongside my precious parchment maps. I was, in short, a geek.

...And the Curse

I mentioned earlier that I went to see Bakshi's movie with an open mind. It was well that I did, and also well that my mind, at that age, was still mostly empty. Having recently completed another viewing of the film, nearly 25 years later, I honestly wonder what I was thinking then. Writing the above paragraphs was very difficult, as I now have almost no recollection of what it was I originally enjoyed about the movie, those many long years ago. Perhaps it was my youthful enthusiasm. Perhaps it was my youthful idealism. Perhaps it was my youthful naïveté. Perhaps it was some mysterious brain tumor from which I have miraculously recovered.

The fact of the matter is that Bakshi's film is not a very good one. After decades of listening to film scores by Morricone, Williams, Elfman, Shore, Knopfler, Copeland, and countless others, I hate to say that Leonard Rosenman's music starts things badly through its lack of subtlety and, sadly, musicality. And most tellingly, Bakshi's animation has not held up well at all. While the human movements in *The Lord of the Rings* are still more realistic than many contemporary efforts (most shockingly bad in *Ice Age*), the animation is wildly inconsistent. The principal characters are saddled with conventionally cartoonish visages (where *did* Legolas get that nose?) while background characters get the full rotoscope treatment.

But the real problem with filming actors and then transferring their performances to animated cels (in essence, the process of rotoscoping) is with the actors themselves. The lion's share of United Artists' budget was spent on animators, not on actors. While the lead vocal characterizations are fine (the acting budget being spent most lavishly in this area) it almost seems that the actors playing minor roles (all the Orcs and the folks at the Prancing Pony, in particular) were recruited from some amateur three-ring circus. Bad performances cannot be improved by animating them. In fact, it might even be a worse choice, since good animators are capable of creating fairly decent performances *from scratch.*

Bakshi's Real Shortsightedness

These minor issues aside, Bakshi's *real* failure is his treatment of the character of Sam Gamgee. Bakshi seems to think that Sam is along for comic relief only, and that the best form of comic relief is Down Syndrome. Bakshi's Sam isn't even really a Hobbit at all, when compared to his fellow Hobbits Frodo, Merry and Pippin. He's just a goofball.

I think this reflects a philosophical shortcoming in Bakshi and highlights Peter Jackson's perceptiveness. Bakshi seems to be too easily persuaded that Aragorn and Frodo—heroic characters, true enough—are the heart of Tolkien's story. They are not. Aragorn, made in the classic heroic mode, is merely a standard by which other heroes in the story may be compared. He's a hero who was born for heroism, bred for heroism, destined for heroism. Frodo, by contrast, is a hero in more of the modern sense: one who, like the British soldier Tolkien himself was, answers the call of duty with determination and faithfulness, but who also returns from the battle somehow not really having been up to the challenge, and broken because of it.

Bakshi mostly gets these two characters right. But he totally misses the simple heroism of Samwise Gamgee, who exhibits the best of the strengths of the common person, the heroism of dealing with everyday life: of being faithful through thick and thin, of rising to great challenges when needed; and of contentedly, if somewhat sadly, carrying on after the great events of life have passed—knowing that all which follows is likely to be somehow anticlimactic. This is a pathos that Jackson and Sean Astin have portrayed in their Sam Gamgee. It is a level of being that Bakshi's Sam, in all his glorious two-dimensionality, could never have approached even if Bakshi *had* raised financing for a sequel. It's just as well that Rankin/Bass picked up the story where Bakshi left off.

So how do Jackson and Bakshi compare?

This is an apples-to-apples comparison, which Jackson wins almost without a fight. To Bakshi's credit, I find the confidence and grim determination of his Aragorn at the Prancing Pony preferable to the angst of Viggo Mortensen's hero-to-be. And as a whole, Bakshi's Elves (Elrond and Galadriel in particular) seem more well-groomed and less dour than Jackson's. For Bakshi, the episode with the Mirror of Galadriel is an opportunity to show the lightness of mind that a 5000-year-old lady might bring to the temptation of the Ring, but Cate Blanchett's Galadriel is all imperiousness and dark night.

Still, in spite of failing to correct many of the narrative weaknesses of the earlier screenplay, and while introducing some new ones, Jackson gives us a film that is satisfying both as entertainment and as art. Bakshi's effort is, sadly, hard to appreciate as either.

❧ Peter Jackson versus Rankin/Bass ☙

JUNE 2002

What were Rankin/Bass thinking?

In 1980, the thinking world was stunned by the free-TV premiere of the Rankin/Bass production of J. R. R. Tolkien's *The Return of the King*. Of course, Rankin/Bass had been regularly stunning the sensibilities of folk everywhere since the fifties, establishing a niche market in stop-motion animated holiday specials such as *The Little Drummer Boy*, *Rudolph the Red-Nosed Reindeer* and *Frosty the Snowman*. Just about any Boomer you meet can hum a few bars of one or more kitsch-tune classics spawned by the musical side of their productions. The studio had even managed to mount a couple of theatrical releases and, earlier in the seventies, had produced the only adaptation of *The Hobbit* yet "filmed."

What was particularly stunning about their latest production was that it made very little attempt to cover for the fact that it began the story of *The Lord of the Rings* with the Muster of Rohan and with Frodo already captured by the Orcs at Cirith Ungol. Worse, the adaptation tried to get away with this narrative affront through the device of "The Minstrel of Gondor," warblingly vocalized by Glen Yarborough. This invented minstrel opens the show with a rendering (did I mean to say rendition?) of the Lay of "Frodo of the Nine Fingers," sung as part of a further-invented birthday party for Bilbo at Rivendell sometime after the

War of the Ring. Considering that the running time of the Rankin/Bass *Return* is 97 minutes, better than half of which is consumed by further Glen-warbling, it is rather shocking that the adaptation had the gall to invent this scene at the expense of cutting so many others. On top if it all, the program got so many stinking things—like their visualization of the Ringwraiths—flat-out wrong.

So why the attempt?

In 1978, the first installment of Ralph Bakshi's proposed two-part animated adaptation of *The Lord of Rings* hit the theaters: hit, and pretty much dropped to the ground. While many Tolkien fans warmly received Bakshi's adaptation, the quality of the animation was spotty, and the film won neither the critical nor the popular support needed to warrant financing the second installment. (To some degree, this turn of events motivated Jackson's insistence that all three episodes of the current effort be filmed simultaneously.) It quickly became apparent within the film industry that the Bakshi saga would be left incomplete. Into the void stepped Rankin/Bass.

So the producers at Rankin/Bass found themselves in an opportunistic pickle. How could they take advantage of this licensing opportunity from Saul Zaentz and still end up with a viable product? After all, Bakshi's version had complicated matters by adapting one-and-a-half of Tolkien's three volumes, covering half the material in *The Two Towers*. The easy option would be to pick up the Gondor/Rohan narrative where Bakshi left off, and match up the Frodo/Sam narrative accordingly. And with this tough decision having been made, on they went to other, tougher choices, alas! making some pretty poor ones, but also making some right moves along the way.

The Rankin/Bass Visuals

One of the happier aspects of the Rankin/Bass production is the background animation. While the character drawings and most of the foreground action is awkward (galloping horses), goofy (teeny-headed women) and even downright insulting (say, the wraiths), the landscapes and cityscapes (such as in Gondor itself) come very close to the style of Tolkien's own watercolors of Middle-earth and remain faithful to the details of the author's minutely descriptive prose. In this regard, the production fares about as well as any, perhaps even surpassing Peter Jackson's.

The Rankin/Bass Spirituality

Opinion may be widely divided about the production's choices in this regard, but one thing must be remembered: *The Return of the King*, as produced by Rankin/Bass, was squarely targeted for children's entertainment. Tolkien's book was written for adult tastes and sensibilities, and while he might have argued that writing specifically for children is an artistically offensive endeavor, he was very much clear that the darkness of *The Lord of the Rings* would find a difficult audience even in the adult market.

So the Rankin/Bass production first brings the moral dilemmas into crisp, bright focus, primarily through songs such as "It's So Easy Not to Try" and "Less Can Be More." Where the good and bad in Tolkien's world can often be murky, the lines are clearly drawn for Rankin/Bass. The child in the audience will have no trouble absorbing lessons about resisting temptation, seeing a job through to completion, or being a faithful friend.

More controversially, God is introduced explicitly into the dialog. More than once, when a particularly disastrous event occurs, Sam calls out, "God help us!"[1] This is a far cry from Tolkien's vague, Elvish ecstatic utterances to Elbereth, and brings the monotheistic underpinning of Tolkien's mythology squarely to the fore. Again, this is for the children in the audience, and perhaps a bonus for parents concerned about the spiritual dimensions of Middle-earth in general, and other adaptations in particular.

How do Jackson and Rankin/Bass compare?

Unfortunately, this is an apples-to-oranges comparison, which Rankin/Bass still loses. To be perfectly fair, the two can't be compared; but to the extent that Jackson meets the expectations of his audience, and to the extent that Rankin/Bass met theirs, Jackson wins hands down. Still, if a parent is seeking a way to introduce children to Tolkien without exposing them to the relentlessly graphic evil of *The Fellowship of the Ring*, or if the children simply must be placated with *something*, there are worse choices than *The Return of the King*. In terms of the moral and spiritual lessons to be learned from children's entertainment, it's pretty tough to beat.

Section Notes

[1] Roddy McDowell in The Return of the King Dir. Arthur Rankin, Jr. and Jules Bass, Perf. Orson Bean, John Huston Rankin/Bass Productions 1980 DVD (Warner Home Video, 2001).

The Fellowship of the Ring

❦ Peter Jackson's Vision of Middle-earth ❧

DECEMBER 2001

The director of *The Fellowship of the Ring* has walked a very fine line between faithfulness to J. R. R. Tolkien's vision and placing upon that vision his own unique stamp, and he has managed to do it, for the most part, consummately. Alternately rushed and elegiac, perfunctory and moving, Jackson's film version of the novel manages to portray the key elements that make Middle-earth a fantasy reader's preferred destination. At the same time, Jackson has lifted some of the lesser themes from the novel into the foreground, presenting some new spiritual ideas to his audience for consideration.

First and foremost, the story remains one of tension between Free Will and Providence. The best of Gandalf's words from the book remain intact—if condensed mostly into one speech to Frodo at the crossroads in Moria—reminding Frodo (and the audience) that, first, there are other hands than our own guiding our fate; and second, that it remains up to us to decide what to do with the time that we have.

Jackson's Unique Stamp

But the first of the elements that makes this uniquely Jackson's picture, and one that works very well, is the emphasis on the temptation of the Ring. Gandalf, Bilbo, Boromir, Galadriel, Aragorn and even Elrond (partly through the Prologue) are all given extended, lingering chances to ponder the significance of the opportunity for unrestrained power. While most of these encounters occur in the book as well, the opportunities that are added (Boromir below the Red Horn Pass and Aragorn at Amon Hen) and the time devoted by Jackson to the other encounters make it clear that the personal response to temptation is one issue with which he hopes to confront his audience.

The second element dominates the closing moments of *Fellowship*, though it is foreshadowed in the extended treatment of Gandalf's visit with Saruman. For Jackson, it doesn't seem enough that Tolkien's heroes persevere motivated by the conviction of things not seen (the biblical definition of faith,[1] one with which Tolkien seems utterly content). Instead, the characters can only go on by knowing precisely where they are headed and why. For instance, Pippin and Merry no longer play an unwitting part in protecting Sam and Frodo. Instead, knowing that Frodo is leaving the Fellowship, they deliberately draw the fire of the Orcs. Likewise, Aragorn, Legolas and Gimli do not go in pursuit of the two captured Hobbits having to guess at Sam and Frodo's fate; they *know*. I doubt that Tolkien would have been enthused at this change. In his vision, acceptance of *not* knowing was precisely part of properly understanding the relation of Free Will and Providence.

The third element comes at the very end of the film, as Sam sinks into the waters of Anduin, reaching out for help. To this point (the exception being very brief sequences in the Shire), Jackson's film has been exceedingly dark. Even in Rivendell it is fall, and the colors are muted; and most of the truncated Lórien sequence takes place in twilight. Why? Where is the light? Jackson answers with a vision straight from Michelangelo: the vision of the hand of Man reaching out to God for Salvation, coming in the form—here—of the hand of another Hobbit assisted by a bright Light. It's an audacious addition to Tolkien's vision, and it works!

From the Printed Page to the Screen

A (mostly) live-action film has been in the minds of many a fan since the days of the first *Star Wars* movie. The ability of cinema technology to blend live-action sequences with CGI and other special effects has finally made the film presentation of even the most fantastic images a reality. So how does *Fellowship* score? Excellent, in most ways. The art direction in general is fabulous (well, it kind of had to be, didn't it?) and certain locations (the Shire, Rivendell and the Argonath, as examples) are terrifically realized. Overall, though, the world of Middle-earth seemed a little greasier than I had imagined it. Perhaps I am revealing my borderline-Boomer status on this point.

Expanded Roles for Some Characters...

It's natural that some details of the plot and characters should change in order to make the transition from book to screen. In past efforts, as in the present, it has been obvious that you just can't pack all those characters into the available screen time. So what do you do? Obviously a lot of them have to go (like Tom Bombadil) and others must be presented as composites. But what's up with the expanded roles for Arwen and Elrond? In Tolkien's *Fellowship* they surface only at Rivendell, while in the movie they become explicitly significant players in the drama. Why? Presuming that expanded roles weren't the price to pay to get the actors Jackson wanted, it's pretty easy to account for Liv Tyler's presence. With the second movie still a year away, you can't really wait until the second movie for Éowyn to appear as the series' primary romance interest. A viable love interest must appear early to give the movie a strong, young, attractive female character, making the standalone-film formula work. It does leave one to wonder, though, what role will actually be left for Éowyn to play as the story progresses. Will Tyler be given less to do in Part II? Hmmm. Regarding Elrond, his newly-visualized

(Prologue) warrior status (though true to the novel) will presumably just simplify things, obviating the need to account for his sons Elladan and Elrohir... We shall see.

...And Reduced Roles for Others

Tom Bombadil is not the only character MIA. There are myriad others. But, as with other adaptations, Bombadil's absence is the most significant, and troublesome. Does he disappear simply because Jackson, like the rest of us, has no clue what Bombadil is to represent? Certainly, Tolkien spent a great number of words on Bombadil for a reason, and it could only have been to clarify things spiritual: for instance, that there are powers in the world over which things material (and even magical) have no influence. Do these spiritual implications come through strongly enough in the movie without Bombadil? Do they need to? Jackson seems to have substituted magically-powered females and Wizard-duels for the role intended for Bombadil. Why do Elrond and Celeborn seem so, uh, reserved in comparison to their female counterparts?

The Performances

It's certainly a pleasure to see many familiar faces from around the world cropping up in wonderful and delightful ways. After *The Matrix*, for instance, it's great to see Hugo Weaving get a turn at ancient nobility as Elrond. Likewise, it's absolute genius to cast Ian Holm as Bilbo. And while other international favorites such as Christopher Lee, Ian McKellen and Cate Blanchett contribute in major roles, I'll go out on a limb here and nominate Sean Astin as the casting coup of the series, and the heart of the film. Ever since *Rudy*, Astin has deserved a shot at anchoring a major film, and here he shines.

The Bottom Line

Though it's clear that this is a darker—and scarier—vision

of Middle-earth than comes across on the printed page, we really don't know about the bottom line yet, do we? Obviously, the film succeeds as terrific entertainment for adolescents and adults, and will no doubt sate the appetite of Tolkien addicts for a few months at least. Box office records will fall, and fall mightily. But what about the entire trilogy? Will it become flabby and perfunctory, like the *Star Wars* films? Or will it actually build momentum, and end with as satisfying a conclusion as the novel? We shall only be able to wait and see, I am afraid.

ᘓ Peter Jackson's Arwen ᘓ

FEBRUARY 2002

The Beauty of the Elves

In J. R. R. Tolkien's novel, Arwen—played with luminosity by Liv Tyler in Peter Jackson's adaptation of *The Fellowship of the Ring*—is referred to as the "Evenstar of her people"[2]: that is, the full flowering of the beauty of the Elves, and yet, by fate, symbolic of their waning. In her veins flows the blood of the greatest of the Elves and the greatest of Men; and as Aragorn first beheld her in the forests of Rivendell, he thought he witnessed through some Elvish magic the very incarnation of Lúthien Tinúviel, the fairest of all Elven ladies that had ever lived. Arwen Undómiel is the daughter of Elrond, granddaughter of Galadriel and Celeborn, granddaughter of Eärendil, even great-granddaughter of Lúthien herself—and distant cousin of her betrothed, Aragorn, himself the descendent of Elros, brother to Elrond.

There is not a doubt that Peter Jackson appreciates the significance of the role that Arwen plays in Tolkien's fiction. The vision of loveliness, strength and nobility that Tyler brings to the screen as Jackson's version of Arwen can leave the viewer no doubt as to the identity of the Evenstar of the Elves. Indeed, Jackson has stronger ideas in store for Arwen than even Tolkien intended.

Why Expand Her Role?

For those who have read Tolkien's novel, it is obvious when watching *The Fellowship of the Ring* that characters and events have either been compressed or trimmed. For instance, episodes at Crickhollow, the Old Forest and in the Barrow Downs are missing entirely, and after Bree there is little appreciation of the weeks spent in the wild on the trail to Rivendell.

So in the midst of the rush to the Ford of Bruinen, the seasoned Tolkien fan will be somewhat taken aback to find Arwen, instead of Glorfindel, patrolling the Trollshaws, and then herself outracing the Ringwraiths to Rivendell. There, of all things, she utters Words of Power to bring the waters of Bruinen down upon the Dark Lord's minions. This is a very different Arwen than Tolkien's, who remains in the background of the action and, in fact, never utters a line of dialog until after the fall of the Barad-dûr.

Aside from introducing some very fine scenery for his male viewers, and badly needed onscreen romance for female viewers, what is Jackson up to?

Seizing the Day

The clues to Jackson's intent can be found in the words he puts in Arwen's mouth: having been introduced in the movie in a speaking role, Arwen can now say anything Jackson wants her to. With her character, there are no speeches or dialog that need to be replicated.

So whose words come out of Arwen's mouth? Not Glorfindel's. The words she exchanges with Aragorn and the Hobbits in the Trollshaws bear no resemblance to the High Elf's words of advice and encouragement. Neither are her words borrowed from Elrond, or others of his household at Rivendell. Significantly, her words also do not come from "The Tale of Arwen and Aragorn," published in Appendix A of *The Return of the King*.

53

In cinema's *Fellowship*, Arwen's words come from the mind of Peter Jackson. He has taken full advantage of the opportunity to say some things of his own.

Arwen and Frodo

In Tolkien's novel, Glorfindel's horse Asfaloth bears Frodo alone to the Ford of Bruinen, and Frodo collapses after resisting the will of the Nine Riders. In Jackson's movie, Arwen bears him across the Ford and is the agent of resistance. There she speaks Words of Power to make the river rise against the Nine. Here, Jackson's choices establish Arwen as one of the most potent powers in Middle-earth, capable of employing the same kind of powers that Gandalf and Saruman later use at Caradhras. (In the novel, the flood is the work of Elrond's wielding of one of the three Rings of Power, with flourishes provided by Gandalf.)

Arwen then kneels over the fading Frodo and says, "What grace is given me, let it pass to him. Let him be spared. Save him."[3] To whom is Arwen speaking? What's this "grace" she's talking about?

If Jackson holds true to Tolkien's intent, the grace extended to Arwen by the Valar (Middle-earth's pantheon) is permission to pass into the Blessed Realm. As one of the children of Elrond, the Half-elven, she is allowed the choice of leaving Middle-earth to dwell in immortality with the Valar, or to remain in Middle-earth as a mortal and suffer death. As Jackson's film would have it, Frodo's eventual passing from the Grey Havens into the West is substitutionary.

According to Jackson, then, Arwen's "grace" is the gift of immortality, and her request is made of the Valar. So what Jackson puts in Arwen's mouth in this scene is the closest thing to a prayer ever uttered in Middle-earth.

Arwen and Aragorn

At Rivendell, Jackson also takes significant time to manufacture a scene between Aragorn and Arwen. First, Jackson is at pains to establish Aragorn's self-doubt. Despite Arwen's assurance to Aragorn that he is not "bound to" the same failure as Isildur, Aragorn replies that "the same blood" flows through his veins, as Isildur's heir: "the same weakness."[4] Why not rather have Aragorn recall in confidence that he is "Estel," the hope of his people, and that the blood of Eärendil and Beren also flows in his veins? Perhaps Jackson is hinting at the effects of Original Sin; regardless, it is Arwen who has the confidence to assert that Aragorn will "face the same evil" and "defeat it." Behind every good Man is a great Elf-lass, I guess.

This says far more about Arwen than it does about Aragorn. As the scene plays out, Aragorn's lines imply that it was Arwen who chose him when they first met, rather than he who pursued her (with conditional support from his surrogate father, Elrond) as Tolkien would have it.

For Aragorn's sake, Arwen has "forsaken the immortal life" of her people, telling him, "I would rather share one lifetime with you than face all the ages of this world alone. I choose a mortal life." And in giving Aragorn her pendant she continues, "It is mine to give to whom I will, like my heart."[5]

The selflessness and sacrifice that Jackson has Arwen explicitly exhibit, in dialog of his own choosing, recalls the words that the Apostle Paul uses in Philippians 2:6–7, saying that Jesus did not consider his divinity something to be grasped, but instead gave it up to become mortal, made in human likeness.

A Key to Understanding Jackson

In the words of Arwen, we find one key to understanding the aims of Peter Jackson. Given the opportunity to have her say anything at all, he chooses prayers and expressions of self-sacrifice.

While some may legitimately find Jackson's film too spiritually oppressive, it's also easy to see how others may find light in the midst of the darkness.

It is there by design.

ஒ Elrond and Peter Jackson's Aragorn ல

MARCH 2002

Elrond the Warlord

For many die-hard Tolkien fans, *The Fellowship of the Ring* will be memorable for its visualization of the Last Alliance of Men and Elves against Sauron. The opening sequence (with voice-over courtesy of Galadriel)—in conjunction with the flashback sequence during Gandalf's conversation with Elrond in Rivendell)—provides the audience with a perhaps unexpected treat of a visit to the end of Tolkien's Second Age. Yet many a Tolkien-steeped eyebrow may be raised at the role that Elrond is given to play in the Last Alliance, and his commentary at the time of Frodo's arrival at Rivendell.

In Tolkien's version of the story (it still seems odd to write such a thing), the Last Alliance is forged between Isildur's father, Elendil, and Gil-galad, the greatest of Elven warriors in Middle-earth. Gil-galad and Elendil both perish in the desperate battle to overthrow Sauron. Isildur stands by his father at his death, while Elrond, as Gil-galad's herald, is by the Elf's side as he falls. Isildur goes to on regain the throne of Gondor, of which Aragorn is the legitimate heir, while Boromir merely waits to inherit his father's position as Steward. Elrond spends the whole of the Third Age guarding Imladris (Rivendell) against the Enemy while counseling, and eventually housing, the Dúnedain, or heirs of

Gondor's twin North-kingdom, Arnor.

Elrond the Lecturer

Elrond's actions and behavior in Jackson's version of the story become hard to explain. Here we find Elrond presented as, perhaps, the very leader of the Last Alliance; as there is no mention of Gil-galad, it is hard to tell. After the fall of Sauron on the slopes of Orodruin, Elrond also ostensibly becomes Isildur's chief counsel, and is apparently miffed to the tune of three thousand years that Isildur did not take his advice: "I was there, Gandalf," he says, as if Gandalf didn't already know.

> I was there three thousand years ago. Isildur took the Ring. I was there the day the strength of Men failed. I led Isildur into the heart of Mount Doom, where the Ring was forged, the one place it could be destroyed. It should have ended that day. But evil was allowed to endure. Isildur kept the Ring.[6]

The one thing which three thousand years has not taught Elrond, apparently, is to speak less condescendingly to his superiors.

He goes on to lecture Gandalf about the brokenness of Man: "The line of Kings is broken. There is no strength left in the world of Men. They are scattered, divided, leaderless." To which Gandalf replies: "There is one who could unite them, who could reclaim the throne of Gondor."[7] That is, Aragorn.

Aragorn the Self-Doubting

Now here we find Gandalf telling Elrond something that Elrond should also know full well, since Aragorn was actually raised in Elrond's household, and was even informed of his true identity as Isildur's heir by Elrond. But then, that was Tolkien's Aragorn: Estel, the Hope of Men, Elessar the Elfstone, foretold by prophecy, by vision and by name; the bearer of the shards of Narsil, and in whom it was said that the might and nobility of Númenor could be seen again. When Tolkien's Aragorn is introduced at Bree, he comes complete with credentials and introductions from Gandalf, even his own rhyme: "All that is gold does not glitter / Not all those who wander are lost..."[8] Jackson's Aragorn, however, only comes with a five-o'clock shadow, a nickname and some clever repartee. We can at least be grateful that Jackson didn't revert to calling him "Trotter," as Tolkien originally did.

Why does Elrond speak so disdainfully of the Man who is pledged to his rough-and-tumble, stallion ridin' daughter Arwen? Why is it left to Legolas to stick up for Aragorn in the Council of Elrond? Why does Aragorn seem so, well, in need of therapy, instead of like Mad Max?

Aragorn the Heroic

One reason, of course, is the usual concern of compact efficiency in the narrative; another is the need to reduce the number of characters; and a third is the need to introduce historical background through the mouths of principal characters. But oddly enough, in a version of Tolkien's story where almost every act of faith is replaced by an act solidly supported by knowledge and fact, Jackson has elected to remove the certainty of Aragorn's fate with a Modern's portrayal of self-doubt. And he has done this because he sees Aragorn as the central character of *The Lord of the Rings*: the third installment is called, after all, "The Return of the King." For Tolkien, Aragorn is heroic because he is a Hero. For Jackson, Aragorn is a hero because he becomes one.

Further Understanding Jackson

Viggo Mortensen, who plays Aragorn, has been questioned about his portrayal, and tells the press that Aragorn is less about "being" and more about "becoming." We certainly see this as *The Fellowship of the Ring* progresses. After Gandalf falls in Moria, the Hobbits collapse in grief outside. It is at this moment that Aragorn takes charge, encouraging Boromir, Gimli and Legolas to keep the Hobbits moving. Even Boromir's attitude toward Aragorn begins to change at this point, and in his dying breath with Aragorn at his side he declares, "I would have followed you, my brother... my captain, my king!"[9]

Again, it is in Jackson's creative choices that we find clues to his intent. Yes, he has left out much of Tolkien's character-defining backstory for Aragorn; but the invention of three key scenes (Elrond's conversation with Gandalf, the grief of the Hobbits outside Moria, and Boromir's death) makes it clear that Jackson's Aragorn is a Man who will have to win the hand of his betrothed. In this way, and through the expansion of Arwen's role, Jackson has managed to turn *The Lord of the Rings* into more of a romance than was intended by Tolkien. Is this for good or ill? That all depends on how much of a purist one is. For me, it makes the story work better as a movie; and I look forward to further transformation of Aragorn, which in turn points to the "transformation by the renewing of the mind"[10] that is possible for all in Christ.

❧ Gandalf and His Hobbits ❧

APRIL 2002

Why the Shire?

In Tolkien's epic fantasy, one of the most appealing aspects of the story is Gandalf's affection for Hobbits. In the original tale of Bilbo and his adventures, Gandalf's presence was not consistent enough to fully comprehend: who is he really, what are his powers precisely, and what is he up to? This is largely due to the fact that Tolkien did not originally intend *The Hobbit* as an extension of his previously invented fantastic mythology. As he was writing *The Hobbit*, Tolkien was not clear in his own mind who Gandalf was or what he was ultimately up to. Certainly, in 1937, Gandalf was not conceived as the primary foe of Sauron (referred to in *The Hobbit* as "the Necromancer"). Of course, fuzziness of Gandalf's character in *The Hobbit* can also be attributed to the fact that the tale is really Bilbo's; and as he had largely completed the tale prior to the War of the Ring, Bilbo *couldn't* have known Gandalf for who he really was.

And that's as Gandalf would have it, too. In *The Lord of the Rings*, we find that Gandalf is particularly interested in the innocence and peculiar resilience of the Shire's diminutive residents. Peter Jackson has done his audience a favor (and has been very true to Tolkien's intent) by demonstrating this special liking for Hobbits in the opening sequence of *The Fellowship of the Ring*. Jackson not only invents a wonderful reunion of Frodo

60

with Gandalf, he even manages to efficiently portray the interesting love/hate relationship that Hobbits themselves have with the Wizard. Audiences particularly enjoy the smile that alternates with a scowl on Mr. Proudfoot's face as the young Hobbits scamper after Gandalf's firecrackers.

Why Bilbo, and Why Frodo?

Of course, Gandalf doesn't associate with every Hobbit, much as he loves them all. Instead, his lengthy association with these distant cousins of humans focuses on one Hobbit-hole in particular: that of the famous Dragon-Burglar, Mr. Bilbo Baggins. Their relationship intensifies at the beginning of the film when Gandalf begins to suspect that Bilbo's attachment to his ring is perhaps too strong and too reminiscent of its previous owner's attachment.

With Bilbo's departure from his own birthday party, Gandalf's attention turns to Bilbo's "nephew," Frodo. At this point, Gandalf's discussions with Frodo become much more serious because by now Gandalf has also ascertained the identity of Bilbo's ring: that is, *the* Ring. And it is the nature of the Ring itself that explains, even to Gandalf, his attraction for these innocent and resilient folk: only they could keep the Ring safe from the enemy, while simultaneously keeping it safe from themselves. The power of the Ring is a seductive evil, and even the Great (Gandalf, Elrond and Galadriel among them) could not long resist the temptation to use it. Oddly enough, Hobbits can. And so Gandalf can see quite clearly that it is Fate, or Providence, that has placed the Ring in the care of Hobbits and, in turn, the Hobbits under his own care.

Why Sam, and Merry and Pippin?

Of course, Gandalf has very little choice but to send Sam along on the quest, after his impertinent eavesdropping outside Bag End's window. But Gandalf also knows that Sam's loyalty (and other strengths inherent in this small people) will serve Frodo in good stead in the days and weeks to come. And when Providence again intervenes to provide Frodo with the mischievous Merry and Pippin as road companions, Gandalf (among others of the Wise) knows enough not to interfere with the Grand Design when the Fellowship is created. And just so: both Merry and Pippin will themselves play significant roles in bringing the War of the Ring to a conclusion.

Why the Mines of Moria?

When the Fellowship attempts its crossing of Caradhras, it becomes clear to Gandalf that Providence has other paths in mind, and he places the decision in the hands of one whose fate it is to carry the Burden: Frodo. So the party chooses the route that Gandalf has long feared to tread: the journey under the mountains through the mines of Moria. Like Christ in the Garden of Gethsemane, Gandalf has had to surrender his own will and take the road less traveled. And, as Robert Frost wrote, "it has made all the difference."[11] While pausing to consider a choice of routes in the mines, Gandalf discusses mercy, among other things, with his friend Frodo. In condensing several of Gandalf's speeches into this scene, Peter Jackson does a timely job of choosing to remind Frodo (and the audience) that it is what we do with the time allotted to us that counts, and time is limited.

Further Understanding Jackson

Jackson knows what he's doing, of course, because the real heart and soul of the first installment of the movie trilogy is fast approaching: Gandalf's fall into the abyss of Khazad-dûm. So Gandalf's words become not only significant for Frodo (and the audience), they also become directly prophetic for Gandalf himself. He knows that the best thing that can be done for those whom he loves is for him to sacrifice himself in a confrontation with the Balrog. Gandalf, to be sure, has no real way of knowing that his act will sacrificially deliver his companions; yet many have observed that Jackson has chosen to have Gandalf disappear into the abyss in the position of the crucifix, arms stretched out in the traditional posture of Christ on the cross. "Greater love has no man than this," Jesus said, "that he lay down his life for his friends."[12] Gandalf and Jackson apparently agree.

Again, it is in Jackson's creative choices that we find clues to his intent. And some of the most telling moments in Jackson's version of the story are those he spends to show us the agony of the Hobbits outside Moria. These are not the tears of mere physical pain; these are the tears of tragic loss. It is to Jackson's credit that he has not only made the special bond between Gandalf and these Hobbits credible enough that their tears are both justified and believable, but that he manages to draw tears from his audience as well. And if some find in Gandalf a Christ figure, I doubt that Tolkien (who despised allegory) would object to a human heart feeling the same kind of emotion for Gandalf's fall that Christ's followers still feel today at the thought of the death of the best Friend that man will ever have.

❧ Saruman, Wizardry and Magic ❧

MAY 2002

Why Wizards?

Wizards are suddenly hot. I remember seeing John Boorman's version of *Excalibur* in 1981 and being particularly numbed by the Arthurian legend. Despite early and memorable performances by Gabriel Byrne, Liam Neeson and Patrick Stewart, it seemed that most audiences agreed. The whole wizard thing was just too dorky for words. Nigel Terry as King Arthur didn't help matters for post-Watergate, post-Jimmygate cynics, of course. Nor did memories of John Cleese's wizard "Tim" in *Monty Python and the Holy Grail* (1975). But suddenly, with the resurgence of interest in *The Lord of the Rings* and the 21st century phenomenon called *Harry Potter* (among other entertainments), the concept of wizardry is once again part and parcel of our cultural fabric. So the questions have frequently been raised: what is wizardry in *The Lord of the Rings*, what did it mean to Tolkien, and what about the movie's presentation of magic?

The first two of these questions are really very easy to address. In brief, the "powers" of Tolkien's universe have a very definite hierarchy. Eru, the One, is the supreme being, a perfect correlate to the one god of monotheistic religions. Under him is an order of created, "angelic" beings: the Ainur. Some of these, the Valar, are given the task of ordering and supervising the affairs of

Arda (our Earth), and are variously described by Tolkien as analogous to the Greek gods, or Catholicism's Archangels. The Maiar—lesser of the Ainur who followed the Valar in their work in Arda—are of a class commonly thought of as "angels" and "demons." While the fact is not explicit in the text of *The Lord of the Rings*, Tolkien's larger mythology makes it clear that Sauron himself—originally in the service of Eru and later a follower of the rebellious Melkor—is one of the Maiar, as are Balrogs and other evil spirit beings, as well as the Istari (Wizards). So in Tolkien's world, the Wizards are not humans with supernatural powers. They are, in fact, supernatural beings. Gandalf and Saruman, then, are angelic representatives of the Divine: one who is faithful and the other (like Milton's Lucifer, or even Lucas' Anakin Skywalker) who has been seduced by evil.

Why Magic?

Magic is a fairly omnipresent feature of Tolkien's books. From Gandalf's perspective, some very simple "tricks" of his trade could be found in his fireworks or in his ability to provide light for the Fellowship as they pass through Moria. One act of which he was particularly proud, however, was the flourish he added to the flood that descended upon the Black Riders at the Ford of Bruinen. Elrond, through the power of one of the Rings crafted by Elvish smiths in ages past, controls the flow of Bruinen (which is not subject, as mentioned previously, to incantations such as that delivered by Arwen in the movie). But Gandalf does add, through magic, the appearance of white stallions galloping amidst the foam of the flood. Of what nature is such magic? Is it akin to the miracles performed by Jesus in the Bible, such as raising Lazarus from the dead? Not at all. Nowhere in Tolkien's fiction does any created being have power of life over death, or the equivalent. In his letters, Tolkien explains frequently that this "magic," which is also practiced by the Elves in imitation of the Valar, is a form of Art. It is the ability to apply knowledge of things as they truly are in such a way that they become

65

transformed in the eyes of the uninitiated. Middle-earth's fireworks are a perfect example: "magic" to Hobbits, but perfectly understandable to a modern audience (or Wizards). The mithril-inlaid gates of Moria are another case in point: the product of the elevated craft of the Dwarves and Elves, but one whose secret has simply been lost and is an impenetrable mystery even in the Third Age of Middle-earth.

Why, Then, Jackson's Saruman?

It doesn't take a genius, then, to see that Peter Jackson has taken some liberties in his presentation of Wizards and magic in *The Fellowship of the Ring*. Two scenes in particular stand out. The first is the seemingly gratuitous "Wizard battle" at Orthanc. While in Tolkien's book Gandalf's imprisonment takes place rather peacefully (if with chagrin on Gandalf's part), it is wholly explainable within the framework of Tolkien's spiritual hierarchy: Saruman is the most powerful of the Istari, and Gandalf must yield to his powers while in his "spiritual space," so to speak. In the movie, however, it might appear that Jackson simply wants to stage a WWF (Wizard's Wrestling Federation) match aimed at the lowest common denominator. Jackson's purpose, though, has more to do with narrative flow and audience satisfaction than one might think. Consider: Tolkien did not write *Fellowship* as a standalone novel, and his villain, Sauron, comes into play only in the full scope of the "trilogy." Jackson's movie, however, must work as standalone entertainment, and so it must have a viable villain. Thus it is that the facts of Gandalf's imprisonment surface in the first installment in the way that they do. In the books, that subplot is revealed out of chronological sequence.

Better Understanding Jackson's Intentions

For me, a second key "scene" is Saruman's creation of the Uruk-hai. In the books, Saruman's devilry all happens in the background. Jackson, however, in order to add tension to the Uruk-hai's pursuit of the Fellowship along the banks of Anduin, brings it to the foreground in all its grisly, fiendish and barbaric creativity. And this is a potential problem because the audience may think that Jackson (and Tolkien, by extension) believes that magic confers the power to create; that is, that those who practice magic, such as Wizards, have powers equal to that of the Creator Himself. Tolkien was at pains to explain that Saruman's actions were a perversion of an existing creation rather than an original, life-giving act. Jackson's visual treatment of the event does not make that clear—perhaps even the opposite. And so it is important that we distinguish Tolkien's intent from Jackson's, and realize that some of Jackson's "errors" have been in the service of narrative effectiveness.

That having been said, we can safely assert that Jackson's magic comes off a touch more supernatural and less "artistic" in tone than Tolkien's (think again of Arwen's incantations at the Ford of Bruinen). As such, it is perhaps worthy of holding a bit more at arm's length.

✺ Tom Bombadil versus Peter Jackson ✾

SEPTEMBER 2002

Who *Is* Tom Bombadil?

One of the most annoying things in the world is having to endure the self-important party chatter of some arcane-knowledge enthusiast who carries on in a manner that clearly communicates disdain for those happening to be ignorant of the subject. The following discussion of Tom Bombadil may, unfortunately, convey much of that same feeling for the general moviegoing public, for while Tom Bombadil is a pivotal character in J. R. R. Tolkien's novel, he doesn't appear—even by reference—in Peter Jackson's movies. So why bring him up at all? Isn't that the critical equivalent of an annoying party guest?

Well, very probably, yes. Hopefully, however, our discussion of Jackson's films has thus far helped to demonstrate how his choices—the minor and major tweaks he has introduced to Tolkien's storyline and characters—help us understand what's going on in his films: what his unique purposes are in presenting *The Lord of the Rings*. In the same way, an analysis of the things Jackson has wholly removed can hopefully yield insight into what elements of Tolkien's vision Jackson finds dispensable, and perhaps why he feels that way. It is arguable that the character of Tom Bombadil represents the most significant such omission to be found (not found?) in the first installment of Jackson's film trilogy.

One of the more chilling episodes in Jackson's movie is the crossing of the Brandywine on the Bucklebury Ferry. In the novel, Frodo and his Hobbit friends do not go from there directly to Bree, but instead pass through the Old Forest on the borders of Buckland. After a short series of misadventures, the group is rescued and hosted by Tom Bombadil, a curious mannish creature who not only dwells in the Forest but also seems to be its master. His bride is Goldberry, "daughter of the River,"[13] and the couple's whole existence seems bound to the Forest and its environs. While visiting with Bombadil—who seems well-informed about the various comings and goings related to Frodo's quest—Frodo is surprised to learn that the Ring has no power at all over old Tom. Further, Bombadil seems to be thoroughly uninterested in the thing.

After the Hobbits continue on their journey, Bombadil is again required to rescue them, this time from Barrow-wights (spirits of evil Men, dwelling in old burial mounds) before they finally get on the road to Bree.

Later, in Rivendell, Tolkien's Elrond says of Bombadil, "Iarwain Ben-adar we called him, oldest and fatherless. But many another name he has since been given by other folk: Forn by the Dwarves, Orald by the Northern Men, and other names beside. He is a strange creature."[14] Gandalf shares that "the Ring has no power over him. He is his own master. But he cannot alter the Ring himself, nor break its power over others... And if he were given the Ring, he would soon forget it, or most likely throw it away. Such things have no hold on his mind."[15] Tom himself says that one of his purposes is to "teach the right road, and keep your feet from wandering."[16] In biblical prophecy, this is a spiritual function: "Your ears will hear a voice behind you, saying, This is the way; walk in it."[17] Of Tom's identity, his mate Goldberry merely states, "He is."[18] This directly mirrors God's description of himself to Moses in Exodus 3: "Tell them 'I Am' sent you." Narrative problems aside, it is therefore difficult to deal with the character of Bombadil. How would a filmmaker portray a purely spiritual being, especially in a film that focuses so much on action?

The Eternal Thing

In one of his letters, Tolkien said, "I don't think Tom needs philosophizing about, and is not improved by it."[19] Since the character is so enigmatic, most readers unknowingly heed Tolkien's "advice" and invest little or no energy in formulating some definitive conclusion about the "meaning" of Tom Bombadil—and it seems to have absolutely no effect on their enjoyment of either the book or the character. Still, it is probably fair to say that Bombadil represents the Eternal. That is to say: within the context of Middle-earth, Ages may come and Ages may go, Rings may be forged and entire populations may be annihilated in the struggle to control them, but Tom Bombadil will always Be, and will always be uninterested in relatively insignificant details (insignificant, that is, in the grand scheme of things). For Tolkien, an eternal presence in *any* story would be important, but especially so in a story of such seeming darkness as that of the War of the Ring.

The Link to Tolkien's England

Also significant is the fact that Bombadil is the only character appearing in *The Lord of the Rings* whose entire literary genesis predates the writing of the novel. As story development proceeded, Tolkien discovered a great many characters whose histories eventually became incorporated into his larger mythology; but only Bombadil entered drafts of the story wholly realized. Why? As Tolkien made plain in another of his letters, Bombadil represents the "spirit of the (vanishing) Oxford and Berkshire countryside."[20] The stories published as *The Adventures of Tom Bombadil* bring Tom's history at least through medieval times, if not the period of Tolkien's youth.

So What Was Jackson Thinking?

Being a New Zealander, Jackson likely has little natural affinity for the Oxford countryside of Tolkien's youth, despite the great pains his production designer took to replicate those environs for the movie's depiction of the Shire. It was aesthetics Jackson was after, not a physical characterization of the spiritual sense of the land. Perhaps, for him, the Hobbits themselves suffice. It is harder to excuse elimination of The Eternal from Tolkien's vision, though. Granted, narrative problems almost dictate that the entire Old-Forest/Barrow-Downs sequence be trimmed from the script. But can't the Spiritual Imperative, which Bombadil represents, be represented by *something*?

Perhaps it will be in the coming movies. Perhaps not. It would indeed be a shame if the darkness of Jackson's vision could not be enlightened by the knowledge that, somewhere in his cinematic Middle-earth, there's a jolly fellow in large yellow boots who has the fullest confidence in the world that all things really *do* work together for good.[21]

Section Notes

[1] See Hebrews 11:1.

[2] J. R. R. Tolkien, The Fellowship of the Ring 2nd ed. (Boston: Houghton Mifflin Company, 1965), p. 239.

[3] Liv Tyler in The Fellowship of the Ring Dir. Peter Jackson, Perf. Ian McKellen, Elijah Wood, Viggo Mortensen New Line Cinema 2001 DVD (New Line Home Video 2002).

[4] Liv Tyler and Viggo Mortensen in ibid.

[5] Liv Tyler in ibid.

[6] Hugo Weaving in ibid.

[7] Hugo Weaving and Ian McKellen in ibid.

[8] J. R. R. Tolkien, The Fellowship of the Ring, op. cit., p. 182.

[9] Sean Bean in The Fellowship of the Ring, op. cit.

[10] Paraphrase of Romans 12:2.

[11] Robert Frost, in The Columbia World of Quotations (Columbia University Press, 1996 Online Edition Bartleby.com, 2001), Quote #23989. 2 July 2004 [www.bartleby.com].

[12] John 15:13, NIV.

[13] J. R. R. Tolkien, The Fellowship of the Ring, op. cit., p. 134.

[14] Ibid., p. 278.

[15] Ibid., p. 279.

[16] Ibid., p. 144.

[17] Isaiah 30:21, NIV.

[18] J. R. R. Tolkien, The Fellowship of the Ring, op. cit., p. 135.

[19] J. R. R. Tolkien, Letters (Boston & New York: Houghton Mifflin Company, 2000), no. 153, to Peter Hastings, 1954.

[20] Ibid., no. 19, to Stanley Unwin, 1937.

[21] See Romans 8:28.

The Two Towers

৯ The Nature of "Story" ৶

In Tolkien's novel *The Two Towers*, Sam and Frodo take a little time to rest and philosophize as they approach Cirith Ungol. They talk about the story in which they find themselves, and about the nature of Story in general. Not surprisingly, Tolkien's Hobbits observe that we don't hear about *all* stories: the unlucky and the unfaithful are not memorialized. No, it's those who stick it out to the end that we hear about, those who persevere to the conclusion of their quest.

Of course, that's not entirely true, nor has it ever been. But it's certainly true of the kind of tale in which Frodo and Sam find themselves. And it's as true of Peter Jackson's movies as it is of Tolkien's books.

Jackson's is a Different Story

Still, Jackson's filmed version of *The Two Towers* is not the same story as Tolkien's. The titular towers are not even the same as those Tolkien emphasized. Jackson has substituted Orthanc and Barad-dûr for Minas Morgul and Minas Tirith. The framework of Jackson's story is provided by the Axis of Evil that hems in and ravages Rohan and Gondor. Tolkien's framework, though, places more emphasis on the battle for right, a battle which is waged in the shadowlands that form between darkness and light.

With a different framework come different details. The storyline of this movie departs from Tolkien's text in more marked and radical ways than did Jackson's previous installment. This comes as no surprise to Tolkien fans, however, as the teasers and trailers for *The Two Towers* gave up many of Jackson's secrets fairly early.

It's Not Just the Plot

So when seeing Jackson's movie, it's no great surprise that Éowyn plays a very different role for Jackson than she did for Tolkien. After all, her voice is featured more, perhaps, in the previews than in the entirety of Tolkien's novel. We know that she goes not to Dunharrow but to Helm's Deep, and she gets far closer to Aragorn than Tolkien ever allowed. And this is only one of many such details that change in Jackson's story.

It's sufficient to say that the well-read Tolkien buff will find plenty to squirm about in *The Two Towers*, if there's plenty of squirm in the buff. But such plot details are really not the measure of any story, much less Jackson's. Plot variations are just the window-dressing for what the story really has to say. Why is Jackson's story particularly worth telling? Why is it particularly worth watching?

It's About Responsibility

In *The Fellowship of the Ring*, we saw a very different Aragorn and Arwen than Tolkien envisioned. In *The Two Towers*, we see more of them, and it's not just more of the same. We also see a very different Théoden, a different Éowyn and a different Faramir. Why are they different? Why has Jackson consistently given us conflicted characters where Tolkien had served up stock types?

Jackson's treatment of Arwen in *The Two Towers* is a good case study. We see more of her influence on Aragorn, both physically and metaphysically. We see more of her in flashbacks, and in flash-forwards. We see more of the tension between her and Elrond than Tolkien included even in his Appendices. Arwen, like other Jackson characters, exhibits precisely what drives Jackson's movies: the tension between being and becoming, and the responsibility that comes with Free Will and the exercise of choice. "You may want to reject what your family has stood for," Jackson's films tell his audience, "but there will be a price to pay if you do." Count the cost, as Jesus warned His disciples, and pay the piper when he calls.

It's About Redemption

It's also no spoiler, even for those who have never read the books, that Gandalf makes a return engagement in *The Two Towers*. Having fallen into the abyss battling the Balrog in Moria, he ultimately emerges crushed but victorious, and is sent back to aid in the defense against the onslaught from Mordor and Isengard. For Tolkien, this was a major event. For Jackson, it's merely a presage of what's to come. Time after time, Jackson's characters appear to fall only to rise again. It's as if Jackson were enthralled by the show-stopping musical number in the middle of Big Idea's *Jonah*, and decided that the God of Second Chances reigns over Middle-earth as well.

Of course, the repeated motif of victory over death points precisely to the evangelium that Tolkien designed into *his* story: the good news of the victory of Christ over sin, the victory of mercy over judgment, the victory of life over death. Even Jackson's Boromir, we will remember, redeemed himself with his valor in defense of Merry and Pippin and with his dying fealty to Aragorn. *The Two Towers* is all about such redemption and sets the stage for *The Return of the King*.

It's About Faithfulness

Finally, and ultimately, Jackson's movie is about the faithfulness to be found even in seemingly broken fellowship. The image of Aragorn, Legolas and Gimli gamely pursuing the marauding Uruk-hai indelibly defines the guiding heart of *The Two Towers*. Because of the chosen framework for his story, Jackson's movie is darker than Tolkien's book. Because of the details that hang from his framework, his movie is more grisly, and may be hard for many to watch, particularly children.

But in the end, Jackson's movie makes a strong case for perseverance, for faithful service to those you've sworn to support; and for standing by the right thing after all has been considered and doubts have been weighed. Do the right thing, Jackson says, and do it whatever the cost.

Anyone, then, who knows the good he ought to do and doesn't do it, sins.[1]

❧ An Odd Place to End? ❧

FEBRUARY 2003

The Big Surprise

Okay. It's time for me to admit one of my personal quirks. (No, not *that* one!) For me, much of viewing *The Two Towers* was very like the moment a friend experienced when watching *The Empire Strikes Back*: "Wait a minute! Either the Millennium Falcon spent an *awfully* long time outrunning the Empire, or Luke's Jedi training with Yoda was really *short*."

Consistent timelines and geography are essential to my enjoyment of a film. So for a great deal of Jackson's second installment of *The Lord of the Rings*, I was squirming in my seat. After all, they'd taken Tolkien's neatly ordered and sensible universe and ground it into hamburger. Why?

Of course, the screenwriters faced a huge challenge because Tolkien's book is neatly divided into two halves that don't cut back and forth between each other—and that approach doesn't work with a movie. Making matters worse, there are really two parallel narratives to the "west" half of the book, making a total of three distinct story threads to follow.

So clearly there was deliberate intent in ending *The Two Towers* where Jackson did. It was no accident that the movie closes with the drowning of Isengard instead of the disaster at Cirith Ungol, but it may have been a big surprise to many Tolkien fans.

Thread One: Sam, Frodo and Gollum

The first of Jackson's major story threads follows Sam and Frodo on the first leg of their journey toward Mordor. At the end of *The Fellowship of the Ring*, they have come into the Emyn Muil, and it is here that they encounter Gollum. Reconciling themselves to the need of his services as a guide, they take a path through the Dead Marshes to the Black Gate. From there, Gollum persuades them to travel south through Ithilien, where Faramir's men capture them.

In a stunning departure from Tolkien's text, the younger son of Gondor's Steward declines the honorable choice given him by Tolkien and instead takes the Ring-bearer by force toward Minas Tirith via Osgiliath. There, in another shocking invention, Frodo comes face to face with the Witch-king of Angmar. In Tolkien's novel, the Nazgûl are wholly ignorant, at this point, of the Ring's whereabouts! But the real capper is this: these events are being played out a full six days earlier than they *should* be. And that's no mystery to anyone who picks up a copy of *The Lord of the Rings*—Appendix B of *The Return of the King* contains a day-by-day breakdown of the story's events.

Thread Two: Merry, Pippin and Treebeard

Meanwhile, of course, the other two Hobbits are spirited away from Anduin toward Fangorn by the odd alliance of Orcs from the Barad-dûr and Orthanc. Éomer's éored butchers the feuding wretches as Merry and Pippin crawl off into Fangorn. There, they encounter the Ent, Treebeard.

Now, what happens to them over the next few days? In the movie, apparently not much—but whatever it is takes place over a much longer period of time. In the book, they spend a night at Treebeard's "home" before going with him to the two-day Entmoot. In the movie, it's not clear at all what they were doing for up to five days. Then the Entmoot takes less than a day, and—shockingly—the Ents decide to do nothing at all about Saruman.

It takes a "clever" idea on the part of a Hobbit to rouse the Ents—never mind how Merry and Pippin would have been able to guess what was really going on at Isengard, much less anticipate how it would affect Treebeard. And again, these concluding events transpire at least twenty-four hours later than they should have according to Tolkien's timeline.

Thread Three: Helm's Deep

Having chased Merry and Pippin across Rohan, Aragorn and his companions follow their friends' trail into Fangorn. There they re-encounter Gandalf, now no longer the Grey but the White. Together, they all journey to Edoras, where Gandalf casts out Saruman's influence from Théoden, who then retakes leadership of his people.

At this point Gandalf mysteriously departs, and Éowyn, rather than lead the women and children to Dunharrow, travels with them—and with the Riders of Rohan—to Helm's Deep. On the way, Jackson invents an ambush by Warg-mounted Orcs. Days later, Aragorn rejoins his companions at Rohan's mountain fortress just in time for the final defensive preparations—and, in yet another odd invention, the arrival of a band of Elves led by Haldir (of Lórien!). Battle ensues; it is climaxed by Gandalf's arrival with Éomer's éored. And it is this force that annihilates the Orcs—*not* the Ents and Huorns. Because *they can't!* They're apparently still busy ripping up Isengard. (And this just scratches the surface of further complications introduced in the extended edition of *The Two Towers*.)

The Cleansing of Isengard

The linchpin of Jackson's climax, though, is the destruction of Saruman's fortress by Treebeard and pals. As the Ents rip up the Isen's mountain reservoirs (still another Jackson invention) we are treated to a reworking of Tolkien's musings on the nature of Story, courtesy of Sam:

It's like in the great stories, Mr. Frodo. The ones that really mattered. Full of darkness and danger they were. And sometimes you didn't want to know the end. Because how could the end be happy? How could the world go back to the way it was when so much bad had happened? But in the end, it's only a passing thing, this shadow. Even darkness must pass. A new day will come. And when the sun shines it will shine out the clearer. Those were the stories that stayed with you—that meant something, even if you were too small to understand why. But I think, Mr. Frodo, I do understand. I know now. Folk in those stories had lots of chances of turning back only they didn't.[2]

Why End This Way?

What Jackson really wants is to end his movie with an image of renewal: a single visual metaphor that will tie together the spiritual healing that Frodo needs, the bright light to counter the darkness of battle at Helm's Deep, and cleansing for the blight of Isengard. So he plays fast and loose with Tolkien's timelines and geography in order to bring us, at the last, to the flood: not only the flood of Isengard, but an invocation of the proto-mythological deluge—or, we might say, God's cleansing of the world in the time of Noah. "A new day will come," the rainbow promises. "And when the sun shines it will shine out the clearer."

"Those were the stories that stayed with you," Jackson tells us—the ones, perhaps, that we heard in Sunday School or from our parents. They "meant something, even if we were too small to understand why." And, in part, Peter Jackson is using his films (and Tolkien's story) to make "sense" of those Biblical stories— for himself, and for us.

ᦉ Haldir at Helm's Deep ᦉ

MARCH 2003

Why Talk About Haldir?

My observations about the ways in which Peter Jackson has changed Tolkien's story are frequently taken as criticisms. In reality, my musings are just as much a criticism of my own tastes—and thereby merely one means of understanding Jackson's intent with *The Lord of the Rings*. My review of *The Two Towers*, for instance, makes it plain that I think the movie itself does a fine job of bringing Tolkien's themes to the screen. It also works very well as a standalone film—though perhaps not as well as *The Fellowship of the Ring*.

As others have often noted, Jackson and his writers not only had the daunting task of presenting the whole of Tolkien's vision (and condensing his books into some nine or so hours of running time), but the three movies also had to be constructed in such a way as to make each succeed on its own. The task is not unprecedented, having been undertaken by both of the *Star Wars* film trilogies—but it is not simple, either. And the middle movie of the three, lacking as it does the proper beginning of the story *and* the ending, is the hardest to make work.

The changes that Jackson has made to Tolkien's story, then, serve as tremendous tools for understanding precisely what the director felt was essential to communicate within the scope of *The Two Towers*. So even though Haldir is little more than a footnote within the scope of the movie, a study of the character proves a classic case for gaining insight into Jackson's story.

Elves and Mortality

Haldir is, of course, an Elf. In Tolkien's Middle-earth, there are Elves and then there are Elves. Some are wise and noble, like Elrond at Rivendell or Galadriel at Lórien. There are also Elves who are less grand, and even secretive or whimsical. Among these are the Wood-elves of Mirkwood, like those that Bilbo and the Dwarves encounter in *The Hobbit*. These Elves exhibit almost antisocial characteristics. They are hardly gregarious, gracious hosts in the manner of Elrond, or serious and imperious as is Galadriel.

There are good reasons for the differences, naturally. Many of the Elves in Mirkwood are Silvan Elves, of a lesser order in lineage and powers. They are also led by Thranduil, a Sindarin Elf. The Sindar—though classed among the Eldar, the "Three Kindred" of the Elves—did not complete the First Age journey to Aman to dwell among the Valar. As a consequence, the Sindar (in general) were not as ennobled as their brethren. In addition, they tended to exhibit the isolationist tendencies of their greatest king, Thingol, a Sindarin Elf of the original Awakening who wedded the Maia Melian and founded the realm of Doriath.

One of the characteristics of the Elves that distinguished these Firstborn of Ilúvatar from the "Followers" was their immortality. While the life span of Men rarely exceeded two hundred years in Middle-earth, Elves could live as long as the earth itself, if they both avoided being slain in battle *and* retained the will to live. At the time of *The Lord of the Rings*, for instance, Galadriel was already many thousands of years old.

The Elves did not entirely, however, find this "immortality" to be a blessing. Often the exiled Elves of Middle-earth found their ongoing existence trying, and referred to Man's mortality as a "gift."[3] While the spirits of Elves and Middle-earth's Men all journey to the Halls of Mandos after death, the ultimate end of

Elves is tied to the fate of the physical earth while the spirits of Men look forward to an infinite future in the presence of Eru.

Elves in *The Two Towers*

Within the scope of Tolkien's novel *The Two Towers*, the sole Elf appearing in the narrative is Legolas. He is Thranduil's son, an Elf of the Woodland Realm in Mirkwood. If we take *The Lord of the Rings* as a whole (and the Fellowship of the Ring as a band of individuals) Legolas represents the Elves *in general* in the joint quest to destroy the Rings—and he is also specifically an emissary of the Woodland Realm, a people rather distinct from those in either Lórien or Rivendell.

Galadriel herself spent many years in the "veiled kingdom" of Doriath under the tutelage of Melian, and the realm of Lórien is similarly veiled. While one of the Noldor herself, the Sindarin influence is still very strong in Galadriel. Her husband Celeborn is a Sindarin Elf of Doriath.

Elrond's people, on the other hand, represent a very different mood and mode of social interaction. Partly Noldorian in heritage, Elrond is also partly of human blood, and was born after the Noldor's exile from Aman. His ties to the race of Men and his close connection to the soil of Middle-earth account for his more open approach to other peoples. The Last Homely House of Rivendell would be unthinkable in Lórien or Mirkwood. When readers lament the lack of warmth in Jackson's Elves, they are missing the lightheartedness that one finds in Tolkien's Elves of Elrond's house. As Bilbo observed, Elrond's house was "perfect, whether you liked food, or sleep, or work, or storytelling, or singing, or just sitting and thinking best, or a pleasant mixture of them all."[4] Alas, the running time of Jackson's films simply allows no opportunity to fully portray this aspect of the Elves.

In fact, when preparing the screenplay for *The Two Towers*—and attempting to make the narrative hang together while working as a standalone film—Jackson's team found themselves in a perplexing position. Sure, fans of the books will know that the Elves were fighting their own battles in Mirkwood and Lórien during the War of the Ring; but how will it be clear to those new to the story that the Elves were integrally involved in the struggle to depose Sauron? Yes, there's Legolas—but he has his own personal reasons for involvement.

Enter Haldir, and the contingent of Elves he brings to battle.

Elves at Helm's Deep

Just prior to the commencement of the Battle of Helm's Deep, Jackson's movie features the arrival of a host of Elvish archers. Since the ranks of the Hornburg's defenders are woefully thin, their arrival is most welcome. Their skill and weapons will be essential to save Rohan from the onslaught of Saruman's Uruk-hai. At the Elvish archers' head is Haldir. Curiously, Haldir's contingent bears greetings from Elrond, even though Haldir is an Elf of Lórien—one of Galadriel's people, not Elrond's.

The choice is a curious one, and difficult. If the Elves had arrived from Lórien, their path would have taken them along the shores of the Silverlode and the borders of Fangorn, a route on a collision course with the road the Orcs must take from Isengard to Helm's Deep. Coming from Rivendell, though (as might be the case given Elrond's greeting), their path would take them across the Ford of Isen—precisely the path the Fellowship avoided in choosing to travel through Moria! In fact, that route would also place them on the very road that the Orcs travel, and only a few hours ahead of them.

Complicating matters is the fact that Haldir leads them. Viewers not familiar with *The Fellowship of the Ring* wouldn't know that Haldir was the Fellowship's guide in Lórien; and they also wouldn't know that Haldir, subsequent to the Fellowship's departure from Lórien, would need to find some route over or under the Misty Mountains to Rivendell (no easy task, as the Fellowship found out) and then, after learning Elrond's message, lead the phalanx from Rivendell to Helm's Deep—*all in just over two weeks!* Since Frodo and company required three weeks merely to travel from Rivendell to the rear gate of Moria, Haldir's host, traveling on foot, seems to have accomplished the miraculous.

So Jackson and company have not made their choices primarily because these choices make temporal or geographic sense. Their reasons lay elsewhere.

Haldir's Death

More than one fan has mentioned that Haldir's death can bring tears to the eyes even after seven-plus viewings. Clearly, the Elves' presence at Helm's Deep—and Haldir's in particular—seems to have raised the stakes of the battle. Jackson's instincts are cinematically correct. But why, exactly?

A couple of reasons suggest themselves. First, even though Jackson's portrait of Middle-earth's Elves is incomplete, his audience clearly perceives the difference between Elves and Men. Jackson's Elves—rather grim and humorless, as some have noted, and certainly not the "Merry People" of Tolkien's books—are nonetheless noble, and rather grand. Jackson has effectively utilized reserve and a lofty air as a shorthand method for achieving what Tolkien accomplished in a more complex manner. So the death of an Elf has an amplified tragic element for many viewers.

Second, Haldir's death serves notice that the struggle for Middle-earth is one shared equally by all its peoples. All of them are willing to lay down their lives in the effort. "Greater love has no one than this."[5]

Other fans suggest that Haldir's death adds depth to Aragorn's humanity. It is he, after all, who calls to Haldir, a distraction that allows an Uruk-hai to slay the Elf.

Yet lost in all of this is the fact that for Haldir, as an Elf, death is really no great tragedy. Elves do not share the fallenness of Men; they do not live in doubt as to their fate. Unless they have wittingly rebelled against Eru and allied themselves with the servants of Morgoth, they have no reason to fear death. Of course, a theological dissection of the differences between Elves and Men (which Tolkien packed into his commentary on "The Debate of Finrod and Andreth" in *Morgoth's Ring*) doesn't enter into Jackson's movies, so the point is rather moot for most moviegoers.

So Why Haldir?

Clearly, when one elects to depart from Tolkien's meticulously crafted storyline—and thereby, his equally meticulous timeline and geographical consistency—one does so for very deliberate reasons, knowing that the choices will be critiqued (and even howled at) by Tolkien's very loyal and demanding fans.

In the case of Haldir and the Elves at Helm's Deep, Jackson's reasons are fairly simple. First, as noted above, he uses these Elves as a device to illustrate the scope of the battle for Middle-earth, the unity of its peoples in the struggle, and their willingness to all pay the necessary price. Second, Haldir's death serves to heighten the emotion of the battle sequence and helps *The Two Towers* work better as a movie.

Most importantly, Haldir's host helps bring out one of the exceptionally appealing facets of the story, whether in Tolkien's novel or Jackson's movies: Middle-earth is a place, unlike our own, where the struggle of good against evil is fairly clear cut. While modern humans spend much of their time dealing with supposedly "gray" ethical struggles (e.g., "If you come to a stop sign in the middle of nowhere, and can see for miles around that no one is coming, do you stop?"), the residents of Tolkien's world are dealing with something much more concrete and of far greater consequence: Sauron wants to destroy all that is good—are we going to stand by and let him, or are we going to help do something about it?

For Tolkien, this clarity of thought and sense of urgency was interwoven with his faith and with his understanding of what is at stake in our own world, spiritually. Perhaps it is so for Jackson as well.

He who is not with me is against me, and he who does not gather with me scatters.[6]

❧ Théoden's Ill Choices ❧

APRIL 2003

Human Will and *The Lord of the Rings*

Last Sunday was Easter, the day on which Christians celebrate the victory of Jesus Christ over the grave. Of course, before the resurrection came the cross. In the Bible, Jesus is brought before Pontius Pilate, the Roman governor of Judea. During the course of his conversation with the Jewish Messiah, Pilate asks, "What is truth?"

Much of the past two thousand years has focused on that very question, with one group or another—Christians of various flavors, Muslims, scientists, atheists and others—claiming to have a definitive answer.

Perhaps more significant is yet another question: What good is truth to which we assent only—if it merely sits on a shelf, but is never used? Arguably, the defining human characteristic may be the ability to act contrary to what we know is good for us, even willfully so.

As a Catholic, Tolkien understood the human capacity to exercise the will—even if it is exercised poorly—to be both a God-given freedom and a servant of Providence: one of the means by which God elects to work out His will on Earth. As I noted in my review of *The Fellowship of the Ring*, Peter Jackson's movies do not abandon these themes. If anything, they are brought into sharper focus—and *The Two Towers*, in particular, addresses the responsibility that comes with free will.

The Man of Action

One main story thread of *The Two Towers* follows Aragorn as he leads Gimli and Legolas in pursuit of the Uruk-hai who have abducted Merry and Pippin. The decisiveness that Aragorn demonstrates in these opening sequences would have seemed out of place at times in the first of Peter Jackson's movies.

While he was a member of the Fellowship, Aragorn was not so much a leader as one of many leaders—even at times a follower. From the time that Boromir falls defending Merry and Pippin, however, Aragorn assumes quite a different posture. It's as if the words of fealty delivered by Boromir's faltering lips finally convince Aragorn that he has the authority to lead—without Gandalf's guidance, without the Ring-bearer's thoughts to be weighed, without the mission of the Council of Elrond to be protected. He is free to act, and act decisively. "Let's hunt some Orc!" he declares, and the eyes of his companions light up. They are ready and eager to follow.

Another Man of Action

The pursuit is a grueling ordeal. The Orcs are moving fast, and they are well motivated. Just to keep pace, Legolas, Gimli and Aragorn must run day and night—and still, Legolas' keen eyes tell them, they remain a full day behind.

In the grasslands of Rohan, a company of horsemen surrounds Tolkien's Three Hunters. Both parties are relieved to find themselves amongst allies. The Riders of Rohan bring Aragorn and company bad news, however. They have cornered and slaughtered the raiding Uruk-hai. There are no survivors.

This éored (mounted fighting unit) of Rohan is led by Éomer, nephew of the King of Rohan. Éomer is also a leader, both willing to act and willing to accept responsibility for his actions. He is consumed, perhaps even rashly so, with a passion for doing what he knows is right, even if it runs counter to official policy. He has been banished, we discover, for running afoul of the King's counsel.

The Man of Inaction

Éomer acts in stark contrast to Théoden, King of Rohan. Wizened and frail beyond his years, Théoden has allowed himself to become a model of inaction—paralyzed by doubt, mesmerized by ill counsel, ruled by fear, captivated by the glamour of past glory.

After rejoining Gandalf in Fangorn, Aragorn and friends find their way to Edoras to seek counsel with Théoden. Gandalf hopes to rouse Théoden from his malaise and persuade him rise against the army that Saruman prepares to send against Rohan.

It's a tall order. Théoden is in no condition to wield a sword, much less lead an army. His forces are in disarray. His son is dead. His best remaining captain, Éomer, has been banished. His shieldmaiden niece, Éowyn, can only stand by and play nursemaid. Théoden is under the dominion of Saruman's will.

The Loss of Will

For years, Gríma Wormtongue has advised Théoden. A spy for Saruman, Gríma has been the instrument through which Théoden has been tamed and aged. In a cinematic tour de force, Gandalf throws off the yoke of Saruman's dominion—and Théoden is rejuvenated before our eyes.

And it is here, once again, that we find that Jackson and his screenwriters have made very deliberate and noticeable changes to Tolkien's story. And again, we have to ask ourselves, "Why?" The answer is not, presumably, that Jackson has no respect for Tolkien. Nor is it that Jackson is incompetent. We would also be lazy to conclude, "Well, it's a movie, not a book. There are bound to be differences. So what?" No, given the range of options that presented themselves, there must be very specific reasons for the changes Jackson has introduced.

Even in this early sequence with Théoden, there are

significant differences. While Tolkien is never terribly explicit about the means that Saruman uses to control Théoden, there is absolutely no indication that Saruman is tangibly aware of Théoden's rejuvenation. In the movie, though, Saruman is literally taken aback by the incident, though many miles away. While Tolkien's Théoden throws off a psychological yoke, Jackson's Théoden, it seems, throws off a spiritual one.

In the Bible, Jesus remarks on this kind of deliverance, which many have interpreted as exorcism. "When an evil spirit comes out of a man," Jesus says, it may choose to return. "When it arrives, it finds the 'house' unoccupied, swept clean and put in order. Then it goes and takes with it seven other spirits more wicked than itself... and the final condition of that man is worse than the first."[7]

Saruman doesn't reenter Théoden, of course. In Théoden's case, though, Saruman's evil influence is still not replaced by anything wholesome—say, the counsel of Gandalf. No. Théoden's state is still horrible, because he still has only his own poor counsel: the very same counsel that put Gríma at his side in the first place. Einstein observed that the level of thinking that gets us into trouble is insufficient to get us out of it. This is a lesson that Jackson's Théoden has never learned.

The Will to Act, Even Foolishly

And so, rather than act quickly and decisively on Gandalf's advice, as Tolkien's Théoden does, Jackson's Théoden does little more than bide his time and brood—even granted that Jackson stacks the deck against him—while offering the pithy equivocation, "I will not risk open war." Aragorn has to deliver the rather obvious news: "Open war is upon you, whether you would risk it or not."[8]

So what's going on? Is Jackson's Théoden made more complex so the role could be beefed up for Bernard Hill? Has Jackson just lost a screw? Not at all. We must remember that certain lessons from the broader scope of Tolkien's novel may be lost or watered down by the creation of three standalone filmed epics. To be true to Tolkien's themes, many of them must be revisited within the scope of each film. Jackson uses Théoden, at the very least, to remind us that the human will is essential to Tolkien's story. While the first film is rife with reminders of our freedom to act, particularly in the face of temptation, the storyline of Tolkien's *Towers* does not provide as many illustrations. In Jackson's Théoden, however, we have a very tangible reminder that we are entirely free to do as we will, even if it is against our own best interest.

More Poor Choices

Jackson's Théoden isn't done, however. Rather than employing a strong offensive tactic, as Tolkien's Théoden does, he abandons Edoras and moves the entire populace to Helm's Deep—putting his women and children directly in harm's way rather than sending them to the safety of the hills. Worse, he seems to take no conventional military precautions to protect his caravan: no scouts, no vanguard, no rearguard. In the context of Jackson's movie, it's no surprise that Théoden, Aragorn and company are attacked by Warg-mounted Orcs, or that they sustain heavy losses.

To top it all off, upon arriving at Helm's Deep Théoden is still convinced that he is there to merely ride out the storm, and that the Hornburg is capable of doing so. Until Aragorn literally resurfaces in the story, there's nobody at the helm in Helm's Deep. Théoden couldn't protect his people from the flu.

A Near Disaster

The results of Théoden's shortsightedness and ineptitude are nearly disastrous. Despite the aid of Elvish archers and the valor of Aragorn and his friends, the forces of Rohan are no match for the host of Isengard. An Uruk-hai suicide bomber leaps into the culvert under the Deeping Wall, and a thunderous blast rips it apart. In the melee that follows, Haldir and countless others die and the survivors retreat into the Hornburg.

When it becomes apparent that all is lost, and the Orcs are breaking down the door to the keep, Aragorn manages to inspire Théoden to lead the final assault. But for Jackson's Théoden, it is not a final act of heroism; it is merely an act of fatalistic desperation.

The *Real* Man of Action

This moment, of course, is the one that separates the men from the boys—and in Jackson's film, that's an important distinction. For Tolkien, men of royalty didn't earn the title: they were born to it, bred for it, destined to be kings from their mother's wombs. Some, like Aragorn, are even foretold in prophecy; some, like Théoden, may be untimely enfeebled; some, like Legolas' father Thranduil, may seem capricious; some, like Denethor the Steward of Gondor, may be led astray by their own lust for power. But all are royal because they are meant to be. They are of proud lineage, they are better men than are their peers, and they command respect because they are who they are.

But Jackson's Théoden does not command such respect. In fact, he really exists almost as a foil for Jackson's Aragorn, who—very much in contrast to Tolkien's nobles—is more similar to you and me: needing to be convinced that he is worthy of a high calling, needing the occasional goad from a friend or trusted counselor to push him to the next level. Are you and I likely to be convinced on our own that "we are God's workmanship, created in Christ Jesus to do good works, which God prepared in advance for us to do"?[9] I rather doubt it.

Tolkien highlighted the providential role of every person, even the smallest, through his portrayal of the Hobbits. Jackson has chosen to emphasize the importance of the common man through Aragorn. And since Jackson has invested so much in this portrayal of Aragorn, it's critical to *The Two Towers* that Aragorn become the hero of the story. More could be said here about Aragorn; but it should be sufficient to suggest that Jackson's choices for Théoden are more about Aragorn than they are about Théoden. Still, Bernard Hill's performance manages to evoke memories of our own inaction.

And we are still left to ponder Gandalf's thoughts, penned by Tolkien himself: what matters is what we do with the time we have been given. How will we exercise our own free will? An abundance of poor choices have brought most of us to where we are now. Isn't it time to start listening to some good advice?

❧ Peter Jackson's Gollum ☙

MAY 2003

Mercy in *The Lord of the Rings*

It's probably worth noting at some point during this analysis of Peter Jackson's *Lord of the Rings* movies that I'm not really concerned about being "right" in my analysis. My primary concern is exercising good judgment in trying to get at the heart of Jackson's films. That is, with something as dear to the heart as Tolkien's work is to many of us, it would be awfully easy—and tempting—to sit back and take pot shots at the various difficult choices Jackson, Boyens and crew needed to make in bringing the story to the screen.

But such armchair-quarterbacking would be neither constructive, merciful nor responsible. And frankly, I think we can find better uses for things on which we spend $800 million or so than turning them into dartboards. Clearly, there's an audience for this stuff—including me—and it's worthwhile trying to figure out what it is to which people are responding, and why. It's also, I think, worthwhile to try to figure out where we take things once we come out of the theatre.

The reason it's worth bringing this up now is because, as I have pointed out in reviews of *The Fellowship of the Ring* and *The Two Towers*, Tolkien's books and Jackson's films both deal very strongly with the issue of mercy—not just the need to show mercy, but also the implications and ramifications of having shown mercy. If the Bible is right, we really shouldn't expect mercy to be shown to us in any greater degree than we are merciful to others.[10]

Hopefully, then, I have been merciful in my treatment of Jackson; and also hopefully, I may expect some mercy where I have not been "right." And with this, we turn to Gollum—the character in Tolkien's work through whom we learn something of mercy.

The Struggle Within

Perhaps the most satisfying part of Jackson's *The Two Towers* is his portrayal of Gollum. Actor Andy Serkis and Jackson's digital effects team have done unprecedented work in not only bringing an animated character to life, but in enabling the character to interact convincingly with live actors. Other movies have, of course, accomplished similar feats, but not with a wholly invented being such as Gollum.

But the most striking thing about Jackson's Gollum is not the technical achievement (though technical expertise is what makes so much more possible); rather, it's the clarity with which Gollum's internal struggle is presented. Gollum is the quintessential tortured soul, and in him we perhaps find a reflection of ourselves. Gollum could well have written these words: "I obviously need help! I realize that I don't have what it takes to do good... I decide to do good, but I don't really do it; I decide not to do bad, but then I do it anyway... Something has gone wrong deep within me and gets the better of me every time. It happens so regularly that it's predictable."[11] Gollum in Scripture? Huh.

Like us, what gets the better of Gollum is himself: his devious alter ego, always there to tear him down and cast paranoid suspicion on others, never for a moment letting him forget who he has been and what he has done.

The Restraint of Judgment

The most significant contribution to Sméagol's deterioration into the pitiful Gollum, of course, is his long failure to resist the temptation of the Ring. Gollum had his character flaws long before Anduin indirectly gave up Isildur's Bane into his greedy hand—but the Ring exacerbated those natural flaws, and over the centuries twisted an already weak spirit into a classic multiple personality disorder. And this is where the genius of Jackson's Gollum really comes into play: the visual depiction of Gollum's crippled mentality is possibly more effective than the verbal depiction supplied by Tolkien.

Sméagol, the half of Gollum still capable of some good (or at least some attempt at loyalty), takes the upper hand for a time thanks to the mercy Frodo shows him. Twice in Jackson's first installment, Gandalf's words instruct Frodo, "Many that live deserve death, and some that die deserve life. Can you give it to them, Frodo? Do not be too eager to deal out death in judgment. Even the very wise cannot see all ends. My heart tells me that Gollum has some part to play yet, for good or ill, before this is over. The pity of Bilbo may rule the fate of many."[12]

So Frodo follows in Bilbo's steps, and Gollum for a time responds, even thinking that he has successfully banished his alter ego.

The Passing of Judgment

Sam, of course, did not have the luxury of hearing Gandalf's advice. He has very different ideas about Gollum, and about Gollum's ability to be true to his word. Of course, one will naturally distrust promises from the same mouth that has once bitten. So Sam sees Gollum's multiple personalities quite clearly, and names them "Slinker" and "Stinker." His application of the latter epithet earns him a reprimand and criticism from Frodo—and he is genuinely puzzled.

And Sam has his own role to play in Gollum's fate. Gollum

is well aware of Sam's barely concealed malice and distrust, and his more twisted side is only too quick to take advantage. It doesn't help that Frodo must become complicit in Faramir's trickery at the forbidden pool in Ithilien.

So the momentary triumph of Gollum's less odious half is over, and the die is cast: he becomes bent on treachery in his lustful pursuit of his Precious.

The Response to Grace

Within the scope of the movies, is it a foregone conclusion that Gollum will prove unworthy of the grace shown to him? Frodo does not seem to think so. At least, he hopes not. When Sam insists that there's nothing left in Gollum but "lies and deceit," Frodo explains he wants to help Gollum because "I have to believe he could come back."[13]

Frodo means, of course, that he chooses to believe that Gollum is capable of reform—and he must choose this belief because he knows what the Ring is doing to his own mind. He fears that if the damage in Gollum is irreversible then his own damage is irreversible too.

So what about us? Outside the scope of the story, in our own very real world, are we worthy of the grace shown to us? When others give us the benefit of the doubt, do we let them down? Do we often expect the best out of those who have let *us* down, or, like Sam, are we justified in writing them off?

That's not the way the Bible tells us that God works. I, for one, am very grateful that Christ did not wait for us to become perfect before dying for us. That would have been a pretty long wait.

Who Is Redeemable?

But back to the movie. What about Jackson? Does Frodo speak for him, or does Sam? Or some combination of the two? Do the lessons learned in the moral dimensions of Middle-earth even have applicability in our own?

Well, unless Jackson introduces some pretty amazing changes in his final installment, we know how the story turns out. Sam's instincts are pretty good, and we find that Frodo's hopes are nothing more than just that. It's probable that, for Jackson, Frodo simply believes what he does because he must—and who would think differently, in his shoes?

As for this world—well, that's another story.

❧ Peter Jackson's Orcs ❧

AUGUST 2003

Tolkien, Racism and Classism

The peoples of Middle-earth are, admittedly, very European. The people of Gondor and others of Númenórean descent are fair-skinned and gray-eyed. The north-men of Rohan are, not surprisingly, Nordic in their fair-haired stature. And the Hobbits themselves, while a bit on the furry side, are very, well... British. The Southrons on the other hand—those of Near and Far Harad—are swarthy and even quite dark-skinned, while the followers of Ghân-buri-Ghân are presented as aboriginal. Men of uncertain descent are at times described as sallow.

Does this make Tolkien racist? To be sure, the humans of Middle-earth tend to be what might today be called segregationist: purity of bloodlines is of tremendous concern to these people, and at the time of The War of the Ring, to be a Númenórean is a source of great pride—and to be anything else is to be, quite frankly, something lesser. But Rohan's separatism, for only one example, is based more on ignorance, fear and mistrust than it is on ideology. And it's hardly surprising that Tolkien, in writing a mythology he could dedicate "to England," would produce a fantastic world that rather mirrored his own. *The Lord of the Rings* takes place in a northerly clime, not an equatorial one.

The stratification of Middle-earth's social classes has also been criticized. Kings are kings, and pawns are pawns—and the twain shall never meet. But again, to be English a century ago was to recognize and accept the significance of bloodlines and lineage: to know one's place in the world and to embrace it. At the same time, a worthy monarch of Middle-earth knows what it is to be truly noble, and that nobility cannot be reduced to station alone. Even the lowliest may be worthy of great honor through loyalty, faithfulness, courage and service—thus Aragorn and Éomer may confer status and position upon mere Hobbits, that peculiar and unique "branch of the specifically human race."[14]

And Just What the Heck Are Orcs?

But the real key to understanding Tolkien's feelings about race is to address the issue of the Elves, and their counterparts— the Orcs. For here we see in Tolkien truly distinct races. But unlike Dwarves, who are also racially distinct from the human family, Elves and Orcs are related races, the Orcs in dark ages past having been corruptly bred from the nobility of Elvish stock by dark powers. Peter Jackson's movies bring this legend into the foreground in Saruman's development of a new breed of Orc, the "fighting Uruk-hai," which he calls the culmination of the ages-long process of corruption.

And here, of course, it would be pretty easy to bring up the charges of racism again. The Elves, though all fair-skinned, are themselves racially stratified as "High" and "Low," with the High Elves at times snobbishly preferential on the basis of dialect and hair color; and, of course, the Elves contrast nicely with the corrupt and dark-skinned Orcs.

But what *are* Orcs, exactly? Tolkien took great pains to explain the nature of Elves. Unlike humans, whose eternal spirit is housed in a fallen, corrupt body, Elves are simultaneously immortal—Galadriel, for only one example, has lived several thousands of years by the time of the War of the Ring—yet bound to a physical fate. Though Elvish spirits (like those of Men) pass to the Halls of Mandos, this is but a temporary and finite residence. At the remaking of Arda (the End Times of Middle-earth), the Elves face an unknown future while the spirits of Men will dwell with Eru forever, joining "in the Second Music of the Ainur."[15]

As corrupted Elves, do Orcs share a similar fate? Are they long-lived liked their nobler, purer kin? Those issues are never really addressed by Tolkien. For what makes an Orc an Orc, as far as Tolkien is concerned, is not the color of what passes for skin or even the nature of what might be called the Orc's spirit— it's what an Orc does, and whom an Orc serves.

The Orcs of Moria

Peter Jackson really does do a fine job of bringing the Orcs to the screen. Unlike Rankin/Bass (which in an apparent homage to the classical origins of goblins put wings on Tolkien's Orcs) and Ralph Bakshi (whose Orcs resemble denizens of a Cecil B. DeMille leper colony), Jackson presents a vision tolerably consistent with Tolkien's. Thanks to prosthetic and digital technology, Jackson's Orcs are also anatomically distinct enough for us to see real connections between the screen and Tolkien's narrative—and there is yet room for the various classes that exist even within the race of Orcs.

The Orcs of Moria, for instance, are the scuttling, clambering breed that seems characteristic of the Misty Mountains, even the more southerly vales. They are fair archers and fight in swarming hordes with the assistance of cave-Trolls. In Moria, they are dominated by the fearsome presence of the Balrog and flee at his coming—and to the extent that the Balrog may be in league with Sauron, they also serve the Dark Lord. While they are a loathsome menace, perhaps best visualized as they clamber down from the shadows upon the Fellowship in the halls of the Dwarrowdelf, their abilities are limited. They are deathly afraid of sunlight, and will even cower and die under its influence. So it is that they do not pursue the Fellowship as it issues from Moria, and Aragorn must remind Boromir that by nightfall Kheled-zâram will be swarming with Orcs.

Grishnâkh and the Orcs of the Field

It's a pity, really, that Jackson can't devote more screen time in *The Two Towers* to the party of Orcs that takes Merry and Pippin captive and lugs them across Rohan toward Isengard. The stripped-down version of the story doesn't allow many questions to be answered. Why are there two breeds of Orcs among the party: Grishnâkh and his fellows, and the Uruk-hai? Why are they in the open country on the west side of Anduin in the first place? Why do they then trek through the unsafe enemy territory of Rohan, instead of heading for the relative safety of the east bank of Anduin toward Mordor?

The answers are really in service to Jackson's fundamental conception of Saruman as a pragmatically hopeless, duped vassal of Sauron rather than the duplicitous aspirant to power that Tolkien conceives. So there is little clue in Jackson's movies that Grishnâkh and company are Orcs of Mordor temporarily and begrudgingly in league with Saruman's Uruk-hai, browbeaten into taking the westerly course. In Tolkien, a contingent of the Mordor Orcs even breaks off from the main party to beat a return to the east; but the Riders of Rohan force them back.

Grishnâkh and the others of the Mordor breed are more affected by the sunlight than are the Uruk-hai. While not as sun-intolerant as the Orcs of Moria, they are still dependent on their own vile brew for sustenance—and are wholly at the mercy of fear and the will of their master to drive them on.

The Uruk-hai

Saruman's Orcs have had all such infirmity bred out of them. They don't scuttle like the Orcs of Moria, and they don't equivocate or quarrel amongst themselves like the Orcs of Mordor. They are impervious to the effects of the sun, and they equal or excel in stature the Elves themselves and their human allies. They are lean, mean fighting machines, and they have but one purpose—to serve the will of Saruman.

103

Issues of servitude and will—whether in Tolkien or in Jackson, but perhaps most clear in Jackson's movies—allow us to define what it is that really makes an Orc "Orc-ish": misplaced allegiance. In the first place, Orcs are mistakenly driven by fear. For Tolkien, a Christian, this is inimical to a sound understanding of one's purpose in the universe: a motivation toward praise and worship of the creator through love, which "casts out fear."[16] Second, Orcs mistakenly revere the creation rather than the Creator. Whether it's Saruman, Sauron, the Balrog or their own Orc chieftains, all these "lords" are the creation of Eru. And all Middle-earth ultimately falls under the sway of its Creator. Neither demons nor wayward Wizards can supplant the intended majesty of Eru.

The Effects of Idolatry

And really, this discussion of Orcs should scuttle charges of racism or classism in Tolkien. Why? Because as far as Tolkien was concerned, Orcs were merely a fictionalization of a contemporary reality. He transformed his war experiences, for instance—the visceral struggle between good and evil—into "another form and symbol with Morgoth and Orcs" pitted against the Elves.[17] Further, in a wartime letter to his son Christopher, Tolkien called the Orcs "as real a creation as anything in 'realistic' fiction."[18] For Tolkien, it was easy to see that adapting the means of the enemy to defeat the enemy—"attempting to conquer Sauron with the Ring," if you will—bears, of necessity, evil fruit: "The penalty is, as you will know, to breed new Saurons, and slowly turn Men and Elves into Orcs."[19] And their fate? Tolkien conceded the possibility that Orcs, like some human residents of our own world, might be "irredeemable"—yet insisted that, in Middle-earth, mercy should be shown to Orcs "even at cost."[20] This noble (if risky) moral vision is distinctly lacking in Jackson's *The Two Towers*.

So even among men of our own time we may find behavior worthy of Orcs: a prime motive of fear instead of love, and an esteem of creation elevated above devotion to the Creator. The net effect is division among men—the root of all racism and classism—where God intended unity. A house divided against itself cannot stand, as Jesus observed. One cannot serve two masters.

Tolkien's Orcs really bring home the issue to us, personally. If we examine our own behavior, what do we find? Love, and devotion to God? Or fear, and perhaps devotion to self? Are we men as we were intended to be, or have we ourselves become Orcs?

෨ Visions of Justice in *The Two Towers* ෫

LECTURE, NOVEMBER 2003

In the *Ripley's Believe It or Not* category of entertainment news was the apocryphal post-9/11 report that New Line Cinema was considering alternative titles for their filmed version of Tolkien's *The Two Towers*. Even harder to swallow was speculation that the World Trade Center towers were specifically targeted by terrorists because of the titular similarity: they were the symbol of Western values and cultural imperialism—and what could be more Western than a billion-dollar grossing series of Hollywood movies?

The connection is tenuous, of course, but significant—not because of what *The Two Towers* may have represented prior to the destruction of the World Trade Center towers, but because of what the movie suggests about the Western response following their destruction. Already, weekly—even daily—losses in Iraq are causing the American public to lose its will in the "War Against Terrorism." But the first flush of lust for justice was strong enough while it lasted, and pushed us toward Baghdad. Was it justified? Is it still?

The public's response to the war in Iraq is as instructive as the public's response to war as depicted in *The Two Towers*—ironically so. While Tolkien's novel was substantially motivated by his own experience in the trenches during World War I, Peter Jackson's *Towers* presents a vision of war and its conduct strikingly different from Tolkien's.

Tolkien, War and Middle-earth

Make no mistake—Tolkien did not stint in his portrayal of the horrors of war. The battle sequences in *The Hobbit* and *The Lord of the Rings* were not only intended to mirror the grimness of battle in our world. Their terror was in fact, said Tolkien, "what gives this imagined world its verisimilitude."[21] That is, war is hell, and always has been. But what is the model for the conduct of war in Middle-earth? When Jackson's Aragorn declares, "Show them no mercy, for you shall receive none!"[22] at Helm's Deep, is he speaking with Tolkien's voice? Or is it a voice pandering to fear and retribution in the wake of 9/11?

To start with, it's important for us to understand that, for Tolkien, war was a necessary part of our reality. We do live in a broken world. Things aren't perfect. Things like the destruction of the World Trade Center do happen. Groups like al-Qaeda do exist. And, in a practical sense, there has to be some response to that. Tolkien knows that, and he wants to depict that. *The Two Towers* and *The Return of the King* both present gruesome scenes of battle. And Tolkien would be disappointed if that did not affect us in some way. But how do we react?

We should also understand that war in Middle-earth is conducted on different terms than it is in our own world. What are those terms? What's the relevance?

We don't have to look very far to find injustice in our society. We have the World Trade Center, we have the Green River Killer, and we have, maybe, a crack house down the street. So what do we do about these things? How do we go about securing justice for such offenses when justice is not being done in the world around us?

Jackson, War and Middle-earth

The conduct of war in Tolkien's book and in Peter Jackson's movies may be contrasted to give us some insight into how we feel today about the issue of social justice. In the movies, we have characters saying things that Tolkien did not have them say. In the battle at Helm's Deep, Aragorn's instruction for the defenders to show no mercy is an interesting line to be sure, and we may have some sympathy with that sentiment. But it's not a line from Tolkien. In fact, in the novel Aragorn does something quite different. The final morning of the battle, he goes out onto the parapet and actually offers the Orcs a chance to surrender. The contrast may be highlighted by comparing the difference between "Do to others what you *expect* them to do to you," and "Do to others what you *would have* them do to you."[23] A model of war in which the conduct of the enemy dictates the terms of the conflict would not thrill Tolkien.

The Return of the King features a scene in the tower of Cirith Ungol in which Frodo is being threatened by an Orc who says, "I'm gonna bleed you like a stuck pig." Sam replies with a sword thrust in the Orc's back, and the line, "Not if I stick you first!"[24] What Jackson presents is an endorsement of preemptive (if defensive) strikes, a foreign policy that the United States has historically avoided on moral grounds. Our nation now reacts preemptively to even perceived threats rather than waiting to be struck first.

Again, these lines do not come from Tolkien. They are unique to the filmed version of *The Lord of the Rings*, and originate with Jackson and his writers. And with the way things are in the world—and the United States—right now, it's natural to see contemporary attitudes injected into *The Lord of the Rings*. The audience is very much cognizant of the war on terror and the war in Iraq, and the terms under which those wars are being conducted.

Tolkien, War and Redeemability

But what Tolkien intended is something quite different. For Tolkien, of course, the Orcs are evil. They are clearly both enslaved and driven by evil. But they are not "Orc-ish," if you will, simply because of who they are and how they were made, but because of *what they do*. Behavior is far important to Tolkien than genes. In fact, Tolkien stated in one of his letters that the way in which we wage war can have an effect on us. War may be a reality in our world, but we still control the terms under which we conduct it; and Tolkien said that the way in which we conduct ourselves can "breed new Saurons, and slowly turn Men and Elves into Orcs."[25] So Tolkien really believed that, in our own world, there were people who were the equivalent of Orcs. But they weren't designed that way or made that way; they had *become* Orcs.

This brings us to the question of redeemability. In a commentary on "The Debate of Finrod and Andreth," one of his later writings, Tolkien talked about the nature of Men, the nature of Elves and the nature of Orcs. In this commentary, he expressed the idea that, in his own mind, he wasn't entirely sure whether Middle-earth's Orcs were redeemable. The door was left open. This is significant because "common sense," by which we guide our everyday lives, tells us that there are people in the world who are not redeemable. If we didn't believe that, we wouldn't treat certain people—Gary Ridgway or Saddam Hussein—in the way that we do.

What does it mean to be redeemable? For Tolkien, the idea is tied up with the idea of mercy. In battle, as Tolkien conceived it, an enemy who sued for mercy was to be granted mercy, "even at cost."[26] What does that mean, showing mercy "at cost?" In Spielberg's *Saving Private Ryan*, we see the issue dramatized very explicitly when a German is taken prisoner. Given the options of killing him or setting him free, the American soldiers debate the merits of showing him mercy. They decide to let him go, taking the chance that he will renege on his promise not to rejoin the battle. That's showing mercy. And the cost? That same German solider is the one who ends up killing the Tom Hanks character at the end of the movie. Showing mercy includes the possibility that the one to whom mercy is shown will abuse that trust and offend again. And *Saving Private Ryan* argues that mercy should not be shown, because the potential cost is too great.

Tolkien does not agree. We show mercy not because it is deserved, he says, but because failing to extend mercy is beneath our dignity. If mercy is a valuable trait, we show mercy because mercy is inherently valuable, not because the object of mercy deserves mercy. So in the conduct of war in Middle-earth, Tolkien wrote, mercy should be shown to enemy combatants—Orcs included—even at cost. Better to die honorably, Tolkien suggests, than to live dishonorably.

Justice in Our Own World

If we care about justice in the world, how we think about ourselves and our fellow human beings is important. We must ask: are there irredeemable persons in this world? Is Osama bin Laden irredeemable? Is Gary Ridgway, the Green River Killer, irredeemable? Is the crack dealer down the street irredeemable? These are not idle questions, for if there are, indeed, people in this world who are irredeemable, the possibility arises that we are irredeemable as well. Perhaps the person who lives next door to us is also irredeemable.

But if Tolkien is right that even Orcs may be redeemable, that opens up other possibilities. If even Orcs (or Gollum) can be redeemed, then there is hope for us all. Despair is not the only option in this world. Maybe there is hope for us. Maybe there is hope for our next door neighbor or the crack dealer down the street. Consider that neighbor, and ask: are we really prepared to live in a world where there are irredeemable people? Isn't that a frightening place in which to live?

Novelist Booth Tarkington said that "egoistic instinct is subtle and glamorous. It can mistake itself for authoritative judgment upon works of art."[27] So am I wrong in finding that Tolkien's mercy triumphs over judgment? Do I read too much into what he intended? Possibly. I'm sure I bring my own unique baggage to Tolkien, just like everybody else.

But it's a question worth asking: Do we maybe expect too little of ourselves, and think too poorly of our fellow human beings?

✤ The Stewards of Gondor ✤

September 2003

The minor characters in *The Lord of the Rings* often provide the most satisfying grist for the mill of spiritual discussions. My article on Peter Jackson's Orcs, for instance, spawned a series of thoughtful and interesting discussions on the nature of the soul, justice and responsibility. Similarly, a couple of Boromir fans "called me to account" a few weeks before that. In my review of Tolkien's *The Fellowship of the Ring*, Book II, I remarked that Boromir's heated encounter with Frodo on Amon Hen revealed the man's "true colors." How hard on folks I must be, these fans speculated—how self-righteous—if Boromir's inability to resist the temptation of the Ring becomes his defining characteristic, overriding his general virtue, honor and selflessness.

My two young friends were right about me, and they were wrong. Like all of us, it's very easy for me to point out the moral failures of others without confessing my own—and that *is* self-righteous. And I most certainly *do* have my own moral failures, as my wife, pastors and close friends can well attest: moral failures that, with God's Spirit, I have overcome to a degree and hope yet to overcome more fully. So Boromir is just like all of us, not different. All have sinned, the Apostle Paul wrote, and fallen short of the glory of God. And unless we accept God's grace and forgiveness, our "true colors" are very much sinful.

But these are not the points I was making with my comment about Boromir. At Amon Hen, Boromir only made plain the intention he had formulated upon finding Isildur's Bane at Rivendell: to bring the Ring of Power to Gondor as an aid in its defense. Though his purposes may have been honorable, he had been a duplicitous member of *The Fellowship of the Ring*, as Galadriel perceived in Lórien. When confronting Frodo at Amon Hen, he openly declared himself against the Fellowship's intent to carry the Ring to its destruction in Mordor.

Why is this an important point at all? Because in Peter Jackson's movies, and in Tolkien's books, a contrast is being deliberately established. Boromir's temptation is not unique, but his failure to resist might be. Other men subsequently have the opportunity to take the Ring: Aragorn, also at Amon Hen, and Faramir in Ithilien. They face the same temptation as Boromir. How do they respond? What is Tolkien trying to say through these contrasts? Is Jackson trying to say something different?

Kings and Stewards

Faramir and Boromir are, of course, brothers. They are the sons of Denethor, Steward of Gondor. They are heirs of the Steward, and Boromir, as a boy, expects one day to also lead the South-kingdom of Gondor, replacing his father as Steward. But what does that mean, to be "Steward" of a "kingdom"? You can't have a kingdom without a king, can you?

Peter Jackson's movie of *The Fellowship of the Ring* includes "historic" sequences featuring Isildur, the Man who cut the Ring from Sauron's hand and later died in an Orc attack near Anduin. Isildur's father was Elendil, the High King of the Númenórean lands in Middle-earth, and ruler of the North-kingdom of Arnor. Elendil forged an alliance with the Elf-lord Gil-galad in order to defeat Sauron; both died in the ensuing battle, and it was Elendil's sword Narsil that Isildur took and raised against Sauron. The shards of Narsil are those that Boromir finds in Rivendell while Aragorn, who is the rightful heir to the throne of Gondor, looks on. How is it that Aragorn is heir?

Elendil had another son, Anárion. The two mighty stone

figures that guard the lower passage of Anduin with outstretched arms are the images of the two brothers, Isildur and Anárion. At Elendil's behest, these two sons shared the throne of Gondor. Anárion, like Elendil, was also slain in the war against Sauron. Following the war, Isildur traveled north to assume the throne of Arnor and was ambushed by Orcs, and the throne of Arnor passed to his surviving son while the throne of Gondor passed to the heirs of Anárion. Over the long years, the North-kingdom declined; but the line of Isildur endured, culminating at last in Aragorn, son of Arathorn, the only remaining heir of Elendil. For the line of Anárion failed in Gondor, and its care passed into the hands of stewards, who were to act as heads of state until a rightful heir should come to reclaim the throne of Gondor—an eventuality so long neglected as to become unthinkable by the time of Boromir's day.

Why Stewards?

So why did Tolkien invent his history in that way? Why does Anárion's line fail? Why not have a king on the throne of Gondor instead of a Steward?

First, stewards are a historic reality for the British. King James I of England, among others, was a Stuart: of Scottish ancestry and steward of the throne of Scotland. James I of England was also James VI of Scotland, a monarchy that, like Gondor's, had failed of succession and passed into the hands of stewards. After a time, the ruling family adopted the surname Stuart, the Scottish form of "steward," to indicate their status. Not surprisingly, many of the Stuarts perceived their role differently from others who sat on the throne of England; for while they may have been Kings or Queens in title, their royal family name reminded them that they were preserving the kingdom on behalf of the rightful rulers, and not under their own presumed authority.

Second, Tolkien was very much interested in the spiritual symbolism of stewardship. The words "steward" or "stewardship" appear over twenty times in the King James translation of the Bible (yes, *that* King James, the Stuart). In the New International Version, by contrast—translated some 350 years later—"steward" appears less than half that frequently, and "stewardship" not at all. Since the time of the Stuarts, the popular understanding of good stewardship has diminished somewhat. The term expresses the spiritual reality that the things that we have are not our own—that they are given to us by God to merely manage for our own good and the good of others. Because God is the true owner of all things, we only act on God's behalf and really have no "rights" whatever when it comes to position or possession—just like the Stewards of Gondor.

The Throne of Gondor

Tolkien builds this concept into the historic reality of Gondor. Denethor and his sons are not Kings, and will never be. As stewards, they merely manage the kingdom in hope of the day that a rightful king may one day be restored to the throne. After several hundred years, though, the stewards of Gondor are justifiably skeptical of a king's return—a situation not unlike our own spiritual condition today. And this is the central spiritual symbolism of *The Lord of the Rings: The Return of the King*.

In both the books and the movies, Aragorn returns from the long-faded North-kingdom to claim the throne of Gondor as its rightful sovereign: the heir of Elendil and Isildur. The king's return is the fulfillment of a prophecy long derided by those who have lost faith. Will the king return to have found his stewards faithful?

In our own world, the Christian faith also prophesies the return of a King: Jesus, the Christ—not an earthly king, but a spiritual king. It is a prophecy long derided by those who can point to over two thousand years of history as proof that this "king" will not return, much as the skeptics of Gondor claimed. But when this King returns—*if* the "Second Coming" of Christ happens, skeptics say—will he find his stewards faithful, or off

115

doing their own thing?

"Believe it or not," Tolkien's books symbolically say, "the king *is* coming." *The Return of the King's* central symbolism is drawn from the Scriptures and affirms them.

The Good Steward and the Not So Good

As *The Fellowship of the Ring* features Boromir, so also *The Two Towers* features Faramir. *The Return of the King* will feature their father, Denethor. So far, though, Boromir and Faramir provide us with a subtle contrast of stewardship. Both act on behalf of their father, the true Steward. But the temptation that presented by the Ring highlights a difference of character between the two sons.

While both Boromir and Faramir understand that it is their duty as protectors of Gondor to do all that they can to bring aid against the enemy, Faramir has no apparent desire to wield the Ring himself. Until it becomes clear to him that Frodo is the one who rightfully bears the burden—while in Osgiliath for Jackson, and while in Ithilien for Tolkien—he merely desires to bring the Ring to Denethor, who will determine its fate or use. Like Éomer of Rohan, however, Faramir is not willing to abide by the letter of the law if doing so means doing the wrong thing. He lets Frodo continue his appointed quest, and then prepares to face the consequences of having done so.

By contrast, Boromir uses loyalty to Gondor as a smoke screen that allows him to harbor and yield to temptation. On the surface, he declares loyalty to the Council of Elrond. In reality— at Caradhras, at the Gates of Moria, in Lórien, on Anduin, at finally at Amon Hen—he both secretly and overtly seeks to guide the Ring to Gondor instead of Mordor. Not surprisingly, Boromir spends most of his time butting heads with Aragorn, while Faramir will later become one of Aragorn's most trusted captains.

Aragorn, of course—the rightful king, who could by position claim the Ring as a royal possession and heirloom—never wavers in the face of the same temptation. Like Jesus, the spiritual king of the Christian faith, he does not consider power "a thing to be grasped,"[28] and himself acts as a servant both of the Council and the afflicted.

The End of the Story

The Fellowship of the Ring, of course, ends with Boromir's heroic death, in which he more than atones for his failings. In his dying words, Jackson's Boromir stirringly pledges fealty to the returning king. The extended edition of *Fellowship* fleshes out Boromir's character, and Sean Bean's portrayal is dynamically sympathetic. Will the extended edition of *The Two Towers* do the same for Faramir? We shall see. Jackson's Faramir seems less noble than Tolkien's, but the same could be said for Boromir, in the absence of the extended *Fellowship*.

What about Denethor? How will he be portrayed in *The Return of the King*? Will his character, Like Théoden's, undergo significant changes in service of Jackson's cinematic vision? Will the contrast between steward and king ultimately become as strong as it is in Tolkien's books? That also remains to be seen.

And what about us? What kind of stewards are we? Do we even acknowledge that we *are* stewards? If we have instead declared ourselves kings and queens of our own lives, what next? How does *our* story end?

> Who then is that faithful and wise steward, whom his lord shall make ruler over his household, to give them their portion of meat in due season? Blessed is that servant, whom his lord when he cometh shall find so doing... But if that servant say in his heart, "My lord delayeth his coming"; and shall begin to beat the menservants and maidens, and to eat and drink, and to be drunken; the lord of that servant will come in a day when he looketh not for him, and at an hour when he is not aware, and will cut him in sunder, and will appoint him his portion with the unbelievers... For unto whomsoever much is given, of him shall be much required.
>
> (Luke 12:42–48, King James Version!)

❧ Saruman, Sauron and Power ☙

OCTOBER 2003

It will come as no shock to regular readers at Hollywood Jesus that my perspective on Tolkien tends to be, shall we say, somewhat unorthodox. That this is so was brought home in a recent communication from a librarian back east who pointed out that my identification of Minas Tirith and Minas Morgul as the titular Two Towers is, at best, only the fourth or fifth likeliest pairing behind Orthanc and the Barad-dûr, Orthanc and the Tower of Cirith Ungol, Minas Tirith and the Barad-dûr, and so on. This took me aback, and I had to wander back in my thoughts some twenty years or so and reconstruct how the Tirith-Morgul connection had gotten so squarely planted in my brain.

The answer, I found, lay in the words of Elrond at Rivendell. At the council that opens Book II of *The Fellowship of the Ring*, the Elven lord recounts the history of Gondor, and the construction of two watchtowers after Sauron's defeat at the hands of the Last Alliance of Men and Elves: Minas Ithil and Minas Anor. Over the centuries, Minas Ithil falls into disuse and, when occupied by fell spirits, is renamed Minas Morgul. Minas Anor, meanwhile, is renamed Minas Tirith. Between the now-warring fortresses lies Osgiliath, battleground of the shadows which play between the light of the setting sun and the darkness around the moon.

Contrasts attract me. Long ago, my mind latched onto Minas Tirith and Minas Morgul as symbols for the struggle between good and evil that forms such a large part of Tolkien's story. My mind also latched onto Osgiliath as the story's central metaphor for the struggle within each of us: the struggle between opposing forces of darkness and light. As dialog on Hollywood Jesus about Jackson's *The Two Towers* developed, another potent metaphor for this struggle came to the fore: Saruman.

A Power in His Own Right

In the interests of economy and brevity, Jackson of course filmed very little of the Council of Elrond as written by Tolkien—even in the extended edition of *The Fellowship of the Ring*. Naturally, none of Tolkien's exposition about Minas Tirith and Minas Morgul appears in Jackson's movies; indeed, Minas Morgul is barely even mentioned in the first two installments. How, then, could Jackson's "Two Towers" be Minas Tirith and Minas Morgul? They couldn't. Jackson's visuals are instead centered on the Barad-dûr and Orthanc. This is well in keeping with Jackson's expanded coverage of the doings at Isengard—from the details of Gandalf's imprisonment to the slashing of Isengard's forests and the breeding of the Uruk-hai.

Oddly, though, what doesn't come out much in Jackson's movies is exactly who (or what) Saruman is. Sure, he's Saruman "The White," and Gandalf shows him many deferences. But the fact is that, in his spiritual nature, Saruman is Sauron's most natural enemy. Like Gandalf and the Balrog, Saruman and Sauron are both Maiar, a lower order of Tolkien's divinity. As the most powerful member of the order of the Wizards, Saruman is (by original design and intent) the most potent active agent of good in Middle-earth, and Sauron is the most potent active agent of evil.

But what happens? Saruman falls victim to temptation—or, as Jackson, et al., would have it, despair and perhaps greed—and becomes (on paper) allied to evil, even breeding the Uruk-hai at Sauron's behest: an "army worthy of Mordor."[29]

A Stooge for Sauron?

At least, that's the impression we get from Jackson's films. As the movies' scripts tell the story, Saruman has fallen prey to the influence of Sauron through the use of the palantír. Funny things can happen when you "don't know who is watching,"[30] as Gandalf belatedly warns. The funny thing that happens to Saruman is that he sells out to the dark side pretty cheap. "Darn!" he thinks, "I guess I wasn't doing much good anyway. Maybe I should team up with the bad guys. After all, if you can't beat 'em, might as well join 'em."

And so Saruman continues his regular conference calls with the Dark Guy, and they develop this really interesting but completely unexplained plan for waylaying the Fellowship. Saruman will send a band of marauding Uruk-hai down to Anduin to bring back the Hobbits alive and... and... Well, they'll cross that bridge when they come to it, so to speak.

But where's Sauron's plan in all this? Why aren't there any of his forces involved in this little soiree? Or are there? There seem to be some in the pack of Orcs lugging Merry and Pippin toward Fangorn, but where did they come from? Where are they going? What were Sauron's instructions? Was Saruman just passing along Sauron's instructions when he coached Lurtz?

The Ring of Power

Regardless of what detail may surface in the extended edition of *The Two Towers*, we can pretty much rest assured that what Sauron intends is to get his hands on the Ring. The Hobbits have it, and Sauron knows that they have it. In Tolkien's novel, the attack on the Fellowship is explicitly coordinated as a joint operation between Sauron's Orcs of the Red Eye and Saruman's Orcs of the White Hand. After Merry and Pippin are captured, the Red Eyes and White Hands even spend some time jawing over the course to be taken—and the Uruk-hai overrule their smaller and less hardy twisted kin.

And here's the issue lost in the subtext of Jackson's films: Saruman has no intention of acting as Sauron's stooge. He is not interested, as Jackson has him suggest to Gandalf, in joining forces with Sauron. Not at all. What Saruman wants—and for what Tolkien has him recruit Gandalf—is to wield the Ring himself, and depose Sauron. And why not? With Sauron's Ring, Saruman would indeed be a formidable opponent.

The Benevolent Dictator

Saruman is close enough to Middle-earth's true deity to know that the Fourth Age will be the Age of Men. And what Saruman wants is to be their protector and benevolent (if standoffish and rather tarnished) dictator. He isn't really enamored of Orcs and Wargs—but he's pragmatist enough to think that the ends justify the means. He'll use even the foulest of creatures if he gets what he wants. So Gandalf's stay-the-course and fight-the-good-fight line of thinking doesn't pull much weight with Saruman, who merely thinks that Gandalf's been smoking too much of the Halflings' pipe weed.

What Saruman really represents, then, is not a Judas so much as a Peter without correction or repentance. He's less an out-and-out traitor to the cause than he is the guy who flinches when the chips are down, or the gal who simply thinks she knows better. He is, in reality, a lot like the average person. On the one hand, he knows what the right thing to do is—boy, does he! It's his whole doggone purpose for being in Middle-earth. But on the other hand, he's got this serious hankering for something he can't get. For him, it's power; for us, it may be another helping of ice cream or perhaps our neighbor's wife. And so we, like Saruman, rationalize and temporize. We play Devil's Advocate with ourselves and get snookered.

The Other Guy

And the upshot is that Saruman loses not only what he sought to gain, but also everything he had in the first place.

Gandalf the Grey, on the other hand, gets the better of his adversary, the Balrog, giving all of himself in the process. He is then "sent back,"[31] "at the turn of the tide,"[32] as Gandalf the White, supplanting Saruman as the Chief of the Wizards. Why? Because he knew what was right, and he did it. He stayed the course; he fought the good fight.

Saruman, by contrast, becomes something rather like the biblical Esau, who sold his birthright for a mess of porridge. It's an interesting parallel, for the Bible tells us that if we, like Gandalf, fight the good fight—if we keep the faith—we also can claim the spiritual birthright of Israel, the one to whom Esau sold out cheap.

That's not a bad deal. I'll take White over Grey any day.

Section Notes

[1] James 4:1, NIV.

[2] Sean Astin in The Two Towers Dir. Peter Jackson, Perf. Ian McKellen, Elijah Wood, Viggo Mortensen New Line Cinema 2002 DVD (New Line Home Video 2003).

[3] J. R. R. Tolkien, The Return of the King 2nd ed. (Boston: Houghton Mifflin Company, 1965), p. 344.

[4] J. R. R. Tolkien, The Hobbit (Boston: Houghton Mifflin Company, 1966), p. 61.

[5] John 15:13, NIV.

[6] Matthew 12:30, NIV.

[7] Matthew 12:43–45, NIV.

[8] Bernard Hill and Viggo Mortensen in The Two Towers op. cit.

[9] Ephesians 2:10, NIV.

[10] "Speak and act as those who are going to be judged by the law that gives freedom, because judgment without mercy will be shown to anyone who has not been merciful." James 2:12–13, NIV.

[11] Romans 7:17–19, *The Message*.

[12] Ian McKellen in The Fellowship of the Ring Dir. Peter Jackson, Perf. Ian McKellen, Elijah Wood, Viggo Mortensen New Line Cinema 2001 DVD (New Line Home Video 2002).

[13] Elijah Wood in The Two Towers op. cit.

[14] J. R. R. Tolkien, Letters (Boston & New York: Houghton Mifflin Company, 2000), footnote to no. 131, to Milton Waldman, 1951.

[15] J. R. R. Tolkien, The Silmarillion Ed. Christopher Tolkien (Boston: Houghton Mifflin Company, 1977), p. 42.

[16] I John 4:18, NASB.

[17] J. R. R. Tolkien, Letters, op. cit., no. 73, to Christopher Tolkien, 1944.

[18] Ibid., no. 71, to Christopher Tolkien, 1944.

[19] Ibid., no. 66, to Christopher Tolkien, 1944.

[20] J. R. R. Tolkien, Morgoth's Ring: The Later Silmarillion, Part

One Ed. Christopher Tolkien <u>The History of Middle-earth</u> Vol. 10 (Boston & New York: Houghton Mifflin Company, 1993), p. 419.

[21] J. R. R. Tolkien, <u>Letters</u>, op. cit., no. 17, to Stanley Unwin, 1937.

[22] Viggo Mortensen in <u>The Two Towers</u> op. cit.

[23] Matthew 7:12, NIV.

[24] Stephen Ure and Sean Astin in <u>The Return of the King</u> Dir. Peter Jackson, Perf. Ian McKellen, Elijah Wood, Viggo Mortensen New Line Cinema 2003 DVD (New Line Home Video 2004).

[25] J. R. R. Tolkien, <u>Letters</u>, op. cit., no. 66, to Christopher Tolkien, 1944.

[26] J. R. R. Tolkien, <u>Morgoth's Ring</u>, op. cit., p. 419.

[27] Tarkington, <u>Some Old Portraits</u> (New York: Doubleday, Doran & Company, 1939), p. xf.

[28] Philippians 2:6, NASB.

[29] Christopher Lee in <u>The Two Towers</u> op. cit.

[30] Ian McKellen in ibid.

[31] J. R. R. Tolkien, <u>The Two Towers</u> 2nd ed. (Boston: Houghton Mifflin Company, 1965), p. 106.

[32] Ian McKellen in <u>The Two Towers</u> op. cit.

The Return of the King

❧ Jackson's Magnum Opus ❧

DECEMBER 2003

Symphonic. I can find no better single word to describe the design, execution and impact of *The Return of the King.*

Conventional wisdom dictates that movie scripts be designed to function in much the same way as a short story; another apt comparison might be the musical form of the overture. And just as most stories are short in comparison to J. R. R. Tolkien's epic, so are most movies mere overtures in comparison to Peter Jackson's unprecedented cinematic achievement. A running time of three-plus hours certainly allows a design reminiscent of a symphony's multiple, distinct movements—even, as in this case, the many "false" endings for which some symphonies are often criticized.

Other classic films of the past, of course, have also felt symphonic—*Amadeus, Apocalypse Now!, Lawrence of Arabia,* even *Saving Private Ryan.* What distinguishes Jackson's magnum opus, however, is that the tempo of his cinematic symphony's final movement is *largo*—very slow. Proportionately, Jackson spends nearly as much time on his denouement—the "wrapping up" of the story—as does Tolkien. And Jackson's daring pace, perfectly in harmony with the spirit of Tolkien, pays off in an uncommonly satisfying and haunting experience.

It's well that audiences have a chance to catch their

collective breath. Sequences of *The Return of the King* stack up as some of the most visceral entertainment ever conceived—too intense, I would imagine, even for many teenagers. The sequence in the Morgul Vale, for instance, had me literally cowering in my seat, even as Frodo himself cowered from the cry of the Witch-king. I would never have anticipated that the Black Breath could be so effectively evoked through film.

And the Battle of the Pelennor Fields fully conveys the scale and horrific cost of genocidal conflict. I was convinced that this truly was a battle to determine the fate of men—a "war to end all wars." The elephant-like mûmakil may have been overdone, and purists—like myself—will chafe at Jackson's treatment of the Black Ships, but the stand which Éowyn takes at her fallen King's side, facing down the Witch-king of Angmar as he sits astride his winged steed, is a moment that makes Jackson's rocky road to Minas Tirith worth whatever distress it might have brought to Tolkien purists.

Still, Jackson knows that the heart of this story is not cities, dark riders or vast armies. It's the Hobbits, and the struggles they face in playing their own small parts in the War of the Ring. Early on, for example, Frodo and Sam discuss their dwindling food supply—which Jackson craftily utilizes to illustrate how the Ring's power can cause Frodo to doubt even his trusty gardener—yet Sam still manages to anticipate "the journey home."[1]

Similarly, Merry and Pippin look forward to the day they can relax "back at the Green Dragon after a hard day's work."[2] So it's a shock to Sam and Frodo—and dismaying to the audience—when they realize they aren't going to need food for the return trip. It's saddening, when Pippin and Merry are separated, to hear Pippin ask, "We'll see each other soon, won't we?" Merry can only reply, "I don't know. I don't know what's going to happen."[3] And honestly, because Jackson has been brave enough to tweak plot points ever since the Hobbits left the Shire, we feel as if we don't know what's going to happen either.

So we are left to work through the Hobbits' despair with them, feeling, like Pippin, that "we have no song for great halls and evil times."[4] All we have is what Gandalf calls "a fool's hope,"[5] as dire times drive men to fell deeds. "Go now," Denethor says as the darkness surrounds him, "and die in what way seems best to you."[6]

But in keeping with Tolkien's vision—with his belief that his art could "rekindle an old light"[7] in the darkness of this world's anguish—the foolishness of hope triumphs over the despair at the ends of pragmatic wisdom. Frodo may well poignantly ask, "How do you pick up the threads of an old life? How do you go on, when in your heart you begin to understand there is no going back?"[8] And that concluding voiceover may justifiably debunk the subtitle of Bilbo's story: "There and Back Again." But that's still not the end of the tale.

"The ships have come to carry you home,"[9] Annie Lennox sings over the closing credits. How will we feel when that day comes for ourselves? Will we feel, as Peter Jackson expressed in interviews promoting *The Return of the King*, that our story has ultimately been depressing—that whatever triumph we have experienced is but a temporary respite from the "long defeat"? Or, as screenwriters Philippa Boyens and Fran Walsh anticipate, will we find freedom and release?

As they worked on the final phase of this film, Jackson, Boyens and Walsh watched a young man be taken from this world by cancer. Was that the end of his story? Tolkien believed in a life after death, a "place called 'heaven' where the good here unfinished is completed."[10] So do Boyens and Walsh, in a way. "The journey doesn't end here," their Gandalf says. Death is "just another path, one that we all must take. As the gray rain-curtain of this world rolls back, and turns to silver glass, then you'll see it… White shores—and beyond, a far green country under a swift sunrise."[11]

And a languid conclusion to a satisfying symphony.

❧ Peter, Pippin and the Palantír ❧

JANUARY 2004

My librarian friend from Nashua pointed out to me the other day that my objectivity, with regard to Peter Jackson's filmed adaptation, seems to have gone by the wayside. I'm afraid he's probably right.

There's something about premieres, press conferences and rubbing elbows with the stars—even having Viggo Mortensen ask *you* for an autograph—that's bound to make a journalist feel more like an insider than an objective voice for the public. It's a process that is seductive, one that is—well, powerful. It's like toying with Rings of Power, or with the palantíri. Of the latter Gandalf says, "Perilous to us all are the devices of an art deeper than we possess ourselves."[12] And I must confess—the art of film is clearly something beyond me. If it weren't, I'd be in Jackson's shoes and not my own. And the power of Jackson's art has no doubt influenced my thinking due to both my attraction to it and my immersion in it.

But what does Gandalf mean, precisely, by what he says? Or, what, perhaps, is Tolkien getting at with the palantíri? And does Jackson treat those fiery orbs differently?

Right off the bat, I'll be very clear—this column will not be an exhaustive treatment of the topic, but merely an introduction. For those more interested in the palantíri, the best resources are Tolkien's chapters titled, "The Palantír" (in *The Two Towers*), "The Pyre of Denethor" (in *The Return of the King*), and "The

Palantíri" (in *Unfinished Tales*). The latter provides the most thorough discussion.

In a Nutshell

One of the most effective and gripping scenes in *The Return of the King* is Pippin's theft of the palantír. Having been discovered in the wreckage of Isengard by Pippin, it preys on his mind. His obsession leads him to "borrow" the stone from the sleeping Gandalf, and he unwittingly puts himself—and the Quest—in jeopardy by exposing himself directly to the scrutiny of Sauron. It is fortunate (or perhaps providential) that Pippin is pure of heart if willful, and that Sauron is misled by what he sees and hears.

Yet the movie doesn't provide as many details as the books do. What are the palantíri, for instance, and where did they come from? Well, they're not "crystal balls" and don't function the same way. Properly speaking, they wouldn't even work if they were moved about during use, as they are in the film. But they *are* like ancient videophones tuned to specific frequencies and viewing directions, and they have the ability to view what's going on at great distance (if the user knows how to control them). They also have huge hard drives attached, so to speak, which can store a complete record of everything they've seen in the past. They were made thousands of years previously by an Elf named Fëanor, and were given to Aragorn's ancestor Elendil. There were seven of them, and when the strength of the ancient kingdoms failed the stones fell into disuse and many of them were lost. One remained at Orthanc, one continued to be housed at Minas Tirith (the stone that Denethor uses), and one fell into Sauron's hands.

Jackson's Plot Point

In the film, the episode with the palantír mostly serves as a plot device to separate Merry and Pippin, and to goad Gandalf into departing Edoras for Minas Tirith. There's no indication in the theatrical release of *The Return of the King* that Saruman is even aware of the stone's presence at Isengard or of its loss—though of course the audience knows, from the previous movies, that he's used it and that Gandalf thought the use unwise. There's also no reference in the film to the stone at Minas Tirith, nor to the role it plays in Denethor's despair. Most notable, perhaps, is the fact that the Orthanc-stone just sort of passes out of the story without further mention. Where did it get to, after that night at Edoras? Did Peter Jackson just forget about it?

Early reports about the planned extended edition of *The Return of the King* make it clear that much of this missing information will likely be restored. And—as I've perhaps too frequently, too vocally and too generously noted—Peter Jackson has had to make some tough choices about what to include in his films and what to cut. With regard to the palantír, I think his choices were pretty effective. Sure, Jackson doesn't include all the details that purists like me really prefer. But if we re-read Tolkien's sequences related to Pippin and the palantír, we'll find something fairly striking: that Jackson does a better job of dramatizing Pippin and his relationship with Merry than does Tolkien.

This is not insignificant with regard to the success of the films. If a great deal of the emotional payoff of the battle for Gondor hinges on Pippin's song for Denethor—and I think it does—we have to concede that this payoff comes due to Jackson's investment in a host of small scenes related to Merry and Pippin, stretching all the way back into *The Fellowship of the Ring*. And this investment includes Jackson's treatment of the palantír and his choice to emphasize Pippin's use of it at the expense of Aragorn's.

Tolkien's Plot Points

Tolkien, it must be said, also uses the palantír to move the plot forward in much the same way that Jackson does, but there's so much more, too. It's fair to say that Tolkien uses the palantíri as exposition for three important plot points: the treachery of

Saruman, the despair of Denethor, and the ascendancy of Aragorn.

According to Tolkien, Saruman meddles with things that he shouldn't. He believes that he can employ the palantír at Orthanc to further his own objectives, and even to selectively reveal himself and his purposes to Sauron. But the art of the stone is beyond him. His will and his powers are inferior to Sauron's, his purpose is corrupt, and, above all, he has no right to the use of the stone. For Tolkien, the palantír is the means of Saruman's undoing—not only because he increasingly falls prey to Sauron's corrupting power, but because he also unwittingly reveals his treachery to Sauron (before the Ring ever leaves the Shire).

Of course, it remains to be seen whether Peter Jackson deals at all with Denethor's use of the stone in Minas Tirith. In contrast to Saruman, Denethor *does* have the hereditary right to use the stone, as Steward of Gondor. So properly speaking, the stone itself is his ally in resisting the will and the corrupting influence of Sauron, who has twisted the use of the stones to his own purposes. "There is nothing," Gandalf tells Pippin, "that Sauron cannot turn to evil uses."[13]

Though "Sauron failed to dominate" Denethor, as Tolkien says in *Unfinished Tales*, Sauron still manages to "influence him by deceits."[14] He reinforces negative thought with negative fact. There *is* a fleet of Umbar's Black Ships, for instance, heading up Anduin, yes. But Denethor is unaware that those ships bring victory in battle, not defeat. Sauron's attention cannot always be on the stones, so Denethor can at times direct it to his own purposes. Often enough, however, the vision is clouded.

For Aragorn, however, things work quite differently. In the first place, he is the rightful heir to the stones. Second, his will is sufficient to contend with Sauron's. Finally, his judgment is sound. His claim to the palantír is enough, for Tolkien, to inspire fealty: bowing, Gandalf says to Aragorn, "Receive it, lord, in earnest of other things that shall be given back." He then cautions Aragorn about rash use of the stone, to which Aragorn responds,

"When have I been hasty or unwary, who have waited and prepared for so many long years?"[15] And so he *does* contend with the will of Sauron, and comes out on top. Tolkien's use of the palantír to emphasize Aragorn's kingly qualities will be an interesting challenge for Jackson and Mortensen.

The Real Lessons

Plot points and character development aside, there are some moral lessons to be drawn from the episode with the palantír.

First, and most obvious, is the difference between wisdom and folly. Whether in Tolkien or in Jackson—and perhaps even stronger in Jackson's case—there is no doubt that Pippin's presumptuous peek into the stone is unwise. Not only does it present a great personal danger to his mind, it also presents a great danger to the Quest and the people of Middle-earth. The lesson? Know your bounds. Don't chafe at them. Earn respect, earn greater responsibility, and in the meantime practice humility. Even Jesus, the Son of God, "did not consider equality with God something to be grasped,"[16] but instead humbled himself. If humility is good enough for Jesus, it's good enough for a Hobbit, and for us.

Second, and a little less obvious, is the fact that when we transgress—"fall," if you're Boyens and Walsh,[17] or "sin" if you're Tolkien[18]—we've no one to blame but ourselves. Pippin wants to claim that he "had no notion" of what he was doing, but Gandalf chides, "Oh yes, you had. You knew you were behaving wrongly and foolishly; and you told yourself so, though you did not listen."[19] So the problem with sin is not whether we know the difference between right and wrong, but purely in what we choose to do with that knowledge. As the Apostle Paul notes, we are "without excuse."[20]

But finally, the big lesson for Tolkien is simply that there are things bigger than us that we can't grasp, that we can't control, and that, if we meddle with such things we may be placing ourselves in grave danger. In Tolkien's mind, no doubt, such things included the mechanisms of war and the workings of atomic physics. Also, no doubt, he was considering things proscribed by Scripture: necromancy, invoking spirits, astrology. The point is not that these things are necessarily evil in themselves, but that, as in the case of the palantír, we can't always be sure of the powers behind such things, whether good or ill—and we are quite likely less well-equipped than we think to resist such powers.

It's fair to ask, I imagine—how immune can we really be to the power of film? Having allowed ourselves to be entertained by it—and entertained well, I might add—can we really remain objective? The voice from Nashua gives me pause...

❧ Peter Jackson's Fools ❧

FEBRUARY 2004

Given Gandalf's affinity for Hobbits, his behavior toward them is sometimes surprising—not as surprising, perhaps, as the moment in Peter Jackson's *The Return of the King* when Gandalf whacks Denethor up side the head, but odd nonetheless. Early on in *The Lord of the Rings*, of course, Merry and Pippin get on Gandalf's bad side by filching his best skyrocket at Bilbo's birthday party, but at that stage Gandalf merely grabs the two by an ear each and assigns them KP duty.

By the time the fragmented remainders of the Fellowship drag themselves through Rohan, however, Gandalf has some less-than-kind words to direct at Pippin. When Pippin absconds with the palantír and is frightened out of his wits by his encounter with Sauron, Gandalf sensitively scolds, "Fool of a Took!"[21]

Granted, Jackson, Walsh and Boyens play a little loose with the text in this scene—okay, pretty darn loose—but the term 'fool' is bandied about with great frequency by Tolkien, too, if not in the same places that Jackson, et al., do so. Pippin, in fact, calls *himself* a fool. And when Gandalf comments, in Pippin's presence, "There was no lie in Pippin's eyes. A fool, but an honest fool he remains,"[22] both word and sentiment are Tolkien's.

Now, in my experience, no one particularly enjoys being called a fool—and a real fool least of all. What are Jackson and Tolkien up to? Why does Gandalf insist on being so down on Pippin?

Fool of a Took

Shortly after arriving at Minas Tirith, Pippin takes up his responsibilities as a Guard of the Citadel, and he and Gandalf look out toward Mordor. Despite Pippin's foolishness (and Gandalf's periodic annoyance with him) Jackson allows them their moment of serious dialog, condensed from Tolkien's text.

Pippin: I don't want to be in a battle, but waiting at the edge of one I can't escape is even worse. Is there any hope, Gandalf, for Frodo and Sam?

Gandalf: There never was much hope. Just a fool's hope. Our enemy is ready, his full strength gathered. Not only Orcs, but Men as well. Legions of Haradrim from the south, mercenaries from the coast. All will answer Mordor's call. This will be the end of Gondor as we know it. Here the hammer-stroke will fall hardest. If the river is taken; if the garrison at Osgiliath falls, the last defense of this city will be gone.

Pippin: We do have the White Wizard. That's got to count for something... Gandalf?

Gandalf: Sauron has yet to reveal his deadliest servant. The one who will lead Mordor's armies in war, the one they say no living Man can kill: the Witch-king of Angmar. You've met him before. He stabbed Frodo at Weathertop.[23]

And Jackson brings us full circle. Weathertop, of course, had also been the scene of great Hobbit foolishness, as Pippin, Merry and Sam unwisely lit a campfire after dark to cook dinner—and when Frodo cried, "Put it out, you fools! Put it out!", Pippin merely remarked, "Oh, that's nice! Ash on my tomatoes!"[24]

And, characteristically, Pippin really *does* "foolishly" hold out hope for Frodo and Sam—even if Gandalf is merely echoing what he's been told by others (as Tolkien notes[25]), not passing judgment on such hope or even agreeing that it's foolish.

Fool of a Steward

But Pippin finally does have to confront real hopelessness. Tolkien and Jackson both recognize the foolishness of Denethor's despair. In the movie, Jackson has Pippin sing for Denethor as his son Faramir rides off to almost certain death in Osgiliath:

> Home is behind, the world ahead
> And there are many paths to tread
> Through shadow to the edge of night
> Until the stars are all alight
> Mist and shadow, cloud and shade
> All shall fade. All shall fade.[26]

It's truly sad to see a Hobbit—and the Steward, too—driven to despair. Is that preferable to foolish hope?

Foolishness in Moria

Of course, the events at Minas Tirith neither culminate nor initiate the Hobbit's loss of innocence. As early as Moria, the entire Fellowship endures (what appears at the time to be) the tragic loss of Gandalf at the bridge of Khazad-dûm. And what leads to this seemingly fatal blow? How is their presence in Moria announced?

In the movie, it's—once again—that fool of a Took. As Gandalf and the others play detective at Balin's tomb, Pippin's literally idle curiosity gets the best of him, and he reaches out to touch an arrow impaled in a rotting corpse. It's precisely the nudge necessary to send the desiccated remains tumbling into a well, followed by a heavy chain and bucket. The Orcs and the Balrog awake. "Throw *yourself* in,"[27] Jackson's gruff Gandalf admonishes.

But is it *really* Pippin's fault? After all, it was Gandalf who led them into Moria—and forces far greater than Pippin block their retreat. And is the tragedy at Khazad-dûm really all that great, in the long run? There can be little doubt that Gandalf is of greater use when he is "sent back"[28] than he would have been had he not fallen into the abyss.

Foolishness in Rohan

When the Orcs take Merry and Pippin captive, the Hobbits manage to demonstrate remarkable resourcefulness. First, Pippin is alert enough to pester the Orcs into caring for Merry's wounds. Then, as the chase progresses, he's smart enough to feign an escape attempt as a means to leave clues scattered on the plains of Rohan. And finally, he and Merry opportunistically flee under the cover of darkness as the Orcs squabble and are attacked by the Rohirrim.

There's much greater foolishness to witness in Rohan than that of the Hobbits—Saruman, after all, thinks he can shake the devil's hand and get away with it; Théoden, over long years, has allowed himself to be blinkered by Wormtongue; and the Orcs manage to let their divided loyalties sabotage their own ill-conceived plans.

Foolishness in Fangorn

Pippin and Merry also fare well in Fangorn. The Ents and Huorns are slow in responding to threats from the east and the west, and their disdain for haste proves tantamount to cutting off their branches to spite their trunks. But this is a well-established pattern for the sluggish Ents, who have, over the millennia, lost the Entwives and (in some cases) allowed themselves to revert to sedentary tree-ishness. Yet right in their backyard, Saruman breeds Orcs and wastefully—even maliciously—harvests the Ents' beloved trees.

Now, Jackson's Ents are a little slower in the uptake than Tolkien's—but the Hobbits' arrival in Fangorn is indeed like small stones (so Gandalf observes) that start a great avalanche. Without Merry and Pippin, it's doubtful that the Ents would have been moved to timely action. In Jackson's version, Pippin is even credited with the crafty maneuver that finally provokes Treebeard. So, who's the fool?

Sensible Foolishness

If we're at all serious about the issue of foolishness in *The Lord of the Rings*, we pretty much have to admit that there's plenty of foolishness to go around. It's definitely not limited to Hobbits, and certainly not just to Pippin.

In fact, it's arguable that a certain type of foolishness—the *seemingly* misguided faith that things will turn out for the good—is something of a virtue in Middle-earth. Why? Not because it makes sense, certainly, because *seeming* foolishness never does. It only seems, well... foolish. But such a faith is a virtue because—when the evidence finally comes in, and the balance sheets are tallied—hope in the greater good is ultimately rewarded. Hope may fly in the face of reason. It may not make any sense, properly speaking; but it's often a more *sensible* course than mere rationality or despair.

Can we expect casualties along the way? Certainly. Can we always be confident in the specifics of the outcome? No. But we *can* be assured that "in all things God works for the good of those who love him, who have been called according to his purpose."[29] Tolkien believed in the God of the Bible, the God who "loved the world"[30]—the God who is "able to do immeasurably more than all we ask or imagine, according to his power that is at work within us."[31]

Now *that's* reason for hope!

✎ Bigger is Better? ✎

MARCH 2004

American novelist Booth Tarkington, writing roughly contemporary with J. R. R. Tolkien, was concerned with many of the same issues as the British author. In 1927's *Growth*, he wrote:

> There was a spirit abroad in the land, and it was strong here as elsewhere—a spirit that had moved in the depths of the American soil and laboured there, sweating, till it stirred the surface, rove the mountains, and emerged, tangible and monstrous, the god of all good American hearts—Bigness. ... Year by year the longing increased until it became an accumulated force: We must Grow! We must be Big! We must be Bigger! Bigness means Money! And the thing began to happen; their longing became a mighty Will. ... We must be Bigger! Blow! Boost! Brag! Kill the fault-finder! Scream and bellow to the Most High: Bigness is patriotism and honour! Bigness is love and life and happiness! ... With Bigness came the new machinery and the rush; the streets began to roar and rattle, the houses to tremble; the pavements were worn under the tread of hurrying multitudes. The old, leisurely, quizzical look of the faces was lost in something harder and warier; and a cockney type began to emerge discernibly—a cynical young mongrel, barbaric of feature, muscular and cunning...[32]

Even two thousand years ago, Jesus knew that bigger barns and new millraces weren't the keys to happiness. And Tolkien saw the growing problem as clearly as Tarkington did, also fearing the transformation of Men and Elves into Orcs. And Tolkien's literary solution, of course, was the "Scourging of the Shire." Ironically, of course, it's precisely because filmmaking technique has reached a new apex of Bigness that a live-action version of *The Lord of the Rings* has become possible. Yet if we compare Tolkien's own sketches and paintings of Middle-earth with Peter Jackson's films, it's pretty easy to see a difference. What's the downside to Supersizing Tolkien, and what's the upside?

Exhibit One: The Mûmakil

Okay, now this is truly one of my pet peeves. Even in the previews, I thought the mûmakil had been overdone. Impressive, though? To say the least. Quite a cinematic creation. But are they maybe *too* big? Let's take a look at how Tolkien described them.

> Grey as a mouse,
> Big as a house,
> Nose like a snake,
> I make the earth shake,
> As I tramp through the grass;
> Trees crack as I pass.
> With horns in my mouth
> I walk in the South,
> Flapping big ears.[33]

The poem "Oliphaunt," which Sam recites in *The Two Towers*, goes on to call the creature "Biggest of all, / Huge, old and tall." And when Sam and Frodo actually encounter one shortly after, it seems to Sam "much bigger than a house... a grey-clad moving hill."[34] Tolkien himself goes on to note in the same passage that "the Mûmak of Harad was indeed a beast of vast bulk, and the like of him does not walk now in Middle-earth; his kin that still live in latter days are but memories of his girth and majesty."

Still, as I watch them in action in Jackson's Battle of the Pelennor Fields, I am reminded that Tolkien said that "fear and wonder, maybe," enlarged the mûmak in Sam's eyes. Tolkien, after all, while acknowledging the mûmak's "great legs like trees," and putting "what seemed a very war-tower" on his back, did not put *four* tusks on him. A minor point, to be sure—but indicative of our thirst for Bigness.

As Jackson's Rohirrim charge the mûmakil, I then cringe—and not only because of the valiant futility of the attack. "Wherever the *mûmakil* came," wrote Tolkien, "there the horses would not go, but blenched and swerved away; and the great monsters were unfought, and stood like towers of defence, and the Haradrim rallied about them."[35] Only two archers, it seems, ventured close enough to shoot arrows at the eyes of the beasts, and both were trampled.

In Tolkien, the mûmakil didn't charge like cavalry, and they didn't decimate the Rohirrim. And then it dawns on me—the similarity between Jackson's battle with the mûmakil and the assault of the Imperial Walkers in *The Empire Strikes Back*. And the scene becomes like cinematic one-upsmanship. Effective, yes—but Bigger! Better! More!

Exhibit 2: The Nazgûl

Despite the fact that Jackson gets the scene at Minas Morgul wrong—in Tolkien, the Witch-king leads his army forth on horseback, not aloft—I cringe every time I see it. No—I cower. Literally. That's the power of the Black Breath, to be sure.

Yet as the Nazgûl wheels away down the Morgul Vale, I still think, "Now, does that thing really have to *that* big?" But again, Jackson's crew gets much of the creature's anatomy right: "naked, and neither quill nor feather did it bear, and its vast pinions were as webs of hide between horned fingers."[36] But Tolkien gave it a beak, not razor-toothed jaws, and rather wisely he saved a detailed description until the battle over Théoden's body. Jackson gives us too much detail of the Nazgûl far too soon and then is forced to up the ante on himself.

Of course, the steed of the Nazgûl—and its wingspan—must

be large enough to bear an armor-clad ghoul, but in Jackson's vision it has to be bigger yet. While for Tolkien they "circled above the City" and remained "out of sight and shot," for Jackson, they've got to be right in the fray—and big enough to pick up and throw mounted riders. Bigger! Better! More!

Exhibit 3: Caras Galadon

Three times in *The Fellowship of the Ring*, Tolkien describes the tree-borne architecture of Lórien.[37] The first instance is a simple "talan" with a portable screen at one side. It isn't even big enough to hold all of the surviving Fellowship. The second instance is at Cerin Amroth, and from the "lofty platform" Frodo is able to get an unobstructed view of far vistas—including Caras Galadon, a "hill of many mighty trees, or a city of green towers: which it was he could not tell." And at Caras Galadon itself, we are told that there are walls and a gate, and a "road paved with white stone." As Frodo ascends to meet Celeborn and Galadriel, he "passed many flets: some on one side, some on another, and some set about the bole of the tree, so that the ladder passed through them. At a great height above the ground he came to a wide *talan*, like the deck of a great ship. On it was built a house, so large that almost it would have served for a hall of Men upon the earth."

So even with Tolkien we get Bigger! Better! More! But still Tolkien is clear that there is a modesty, simplicity and spareness to the dwellings of Lórien—not the opulent grandeur of Jackson's version. Even at Caras Galadon, the ascent is made by *ladder*, single file, not by the grand staircase in Jackson's movie. And I wonder if the tree dwellings of George Lucas' Ewoks forced Jackson's hand.

Exhibit 4: Rivendell

But the most egregious example in the whole series is Rivendell. Several times Tolkien drew and painted Rivendell—and in each instance, it's literally "The Last Homely House." An apparently single, isolated building—large, no doubt, once you got close to it. But Jackson's Rivendell? Bigger! Better! More!

"So what's the upside?" you ask. After all, it seems I'm doing nothing but carping about the details of a grand work of art. I *did* say there was an upside, didn't I? Well, what is it, then?

And Here's the Upside

Jackson's next picture is one he's been working on for years—*King Kong*. What better project for a director who excels at—is even obsessed by—Bigness? And to a certain extent, Tolkien's story *does* demand an aptitude for Bigness. Peter Jackson really was, in my opinion, the right director for the job.

It does take an aptitude for Bigness to convey the scope and breadth of Middle-earth. Was Moria overdone? No. Was Isengard overdone? No. Were the Argonath overdone? No. Were Edoras and Helm's Deep overdone? Not at all—even understated, perhaps.

And when we come to Minas Tirith, and the Battle of the Pelennor Fields, I think (for the most part) that Jackson gets the scope just right. The size of the armies and the size of the battle are right. The terrible cost of genocidal battle is captured. Heroes die. The devastation is palpable.

Now, I've talked to people who find all the violence excessive, and oppressive. Many have made the same comment about Gibson's *The Passion of the Christ*. But if we want to capture Tolkien, that's a road we've got to go down—because Tolkien knew what he was talking about. He'd seen the horror of war first-hand. And as he explained in his essay "On Fairy Stories," he knew that "dyscatastrophe"—real danger, sorrow and grief—are necessary to "eucatastrophe"—the joy of deliverance. You don't get the resurrection without the crucifixion, Tolkien observed.

And *that's* a bigger, better idea.

᧞ Death and the Swift Sunrise ᧞

APRIL 2004

One of the more memorable moments in *The Return of the King* comes in the heat of pitched battle—but it's not the hurtling energy of siege engines, the digital agility of Legolas on a mûmak, or the rushing onslaught of the Rohirrim. No. It's a quiet moment behind the parapets of Minas Tirith, after the gates have been breached and as Trolls hammer the portal of the city's second circle. It's a lull prior to impending doom, and Pippin says to Gandalf, "I didn't think it would end this way."

"End?" asks a surprised Gandalf. "The journey doesn't end here. Death is just another path, one we all must take."[38]

In interviews last December, Philippa Boyens and Fran Walsh were particularly proud of how this moment in the film plays—its timing and its execution. Members of the religious press, of course, were pleasantly surprised to find an explicitly positive discussion of death in the movie. They asked whether the scripting was a conscious choice. "It's definitely deliberately done," said Boyens. "But what I loved is that Ian McKellen made you feel good about it."[39]

And what are the words that Boyens and Walsh put in McKellen's mouth? The exchange between Pippin and Gandalf continues as follows:

> Gandalf: The grey rain-curtain of this world rolls back, and all turns to silver glass. And then you see it.

144

Pippin: What? Gandalf? See what?
Gandalf: White shores—and beyond, a far green country
             under a swift sunrise.
Pippin: Well, that isn't so bad.
Gandalf: No, no it isn't.

Quite a consolation in the midst of battle. And it reflects the hopefulness of Boyens and Walsh regarding death. As they were wrapping work on *The Return of the King*, they witnessed the last days of friend and young Kiwi filmmaker Cameron Duncan— "watching him come to terms with the knowledge of his impending death," said Walsh. The real-life experience meshed with cinema. "I felt very strongly," Walsh continued, that in the films death is "not a negative thing."[40]

Leaving entirely aside the observation that death, for the enemy, is presumably *not* a positive thing, how is death portrayed in Jackson's films?

The Death of Boromir

The only principal character to die in *The Fellowship of the Ring* is Boromir of Gondor. From the Council of Elrond on, it's clear that Boromir is the Fellowship's weakest link. At the Council, it is decided that the Ring should be destroyed. "If this is indeed the will of the council," says Boromir, "then Gondor will see it done."[41] Yet Boromir submits to the decision begrudgingly. Ascending the Redhorn Pass, Boromir returns Frodo's dropped Ring, rather unconvincingly declaring, "As you wish. I care not."[42] In the extended edition, Gandalf warns Frodo as they approach Moria: "You must be careful now. Evil will be drawn to you from outside the Fellowship. And, I fear, from within."[43] At that moment, Boromir brushes ominously past them. And in Lórien, Galadriel tells Frodo, "The Fellowship is breaking. It has already begun. He will try to take the Ring. You know of whom I speak. One by one it will destroy them all."[44] Boromir himself perceives the accusing insight of the far-seeing Lady of the Mirror.

145

And at the last, on Amon Hen, Boromir finally does confront Frodo, losing his self-control and attempting to take the Ring by force. But somehow, our sympathies are with Boromir. We know, of course, that we would probably be no more likely than Boromir to resist the Ring. There's more to it than that, though: Boromir redeems himself with his valiant defense of Merry and Pippin, and his death is perhaps the most moving moment in the film.

"Frodo, where is Frodo?"[45] the dying Boromir asks of Aragorn.

Aragorn: I let Frodo go.
Boromir: Then you did what I could not. I tried to take the Ring from him.
Aragorn: The Ring is beyond our reach now.
Boromir: Forgive me, I did not see it. I have failed you all.
Aragorn: No, Boromir, you fought bravely! You have kept your honor.

As he dies, Boromir proves not only a loyal subject—"I would have followed you my brother, my captain, my king!"—he is also an unwitting agent of Providence, being precisely the goad that Frodo needs to forsake the Fellowship and set out on his own path. For Boromir, death is heroic; it is redemptive, gallant and noble. Not a negative thing in the least, for a warrior.

The Death of Haldir

None of the principal characters, of course, dies in *The Two Towers*. Jackson, Walsh and Boyens go to great lengths, however, to put Haldir in harm's way at Helm's Deep. Elsewhere I've documented the logistical difficulties of getting an Elf of Lórien to the climactic battle of the second film. Here, it's sufficient to point out that such temporal and geographical gymnastics herald the significance of Haldir's presence.

It's interesting that the extended edition of *The Fellowship of the Ring* gives us a little more time with Haldir in Lórien. He graciously welcomes Legolas, acknowledging his father

Thranduil, and greets Aragorn as a known traveler. Yet there's still precious little screen time for Haldir—so when he shows up at Helm's Deep in *The Two Towers*, we almost expect to see him wearing one of the red shirts from *Star Trek*. Why then are we so moved by his almost predictable death?

Part of the reason is to be found in what Elves represent in Jackson's films. "One of the things that's in Tolkien's book too," the director has remarked, "is this feeling that the Elves are this perfect race. They're intelligent, they're sophisticated... They're spiritual. If you have the Elves in charge of the world, there will be no wars, there will be no hatred."[46] Whether we theoretically agree with Jackson's assessment of Tolkien's Elves or not, the sense of them that Jackson describes certainly comes across in his films. So we naturally grieve at the loss of something so noble and pure.

Jackson stacks the deck, too, by placing women and children in jeopardy at Helm's Deep—and the extended edition ups the ante with extra shots of the distraught and frightened. Tension builds, and our emotions are on edge.

But what's the significance of Haldir's death, in the context of the film? It's perhaps best described by the text that accompanies the trailer for *The Return of the King*: "There can be no triumph without loss, no victory without suffering, no freedom without sacrifice."[47] Haldir's death is loss, suffering and sacrifice. But we know that on the other side of the balance sheet there's triumph, victory and freedom: not a negative thing at all, in the big picture.

The "Death" of Frodo

Oddly enough, some of this goes akimbo in *The Return of the King*—not in a bad way, really, just a rather strange one. In the death of Théoden we do, after all, get affirmation of the lessons learned from the previous films: the redemptive power of valorous sacrifice, and the acknowledgment of victory on the other side. But the denouement, for Jackson, is about something surprisingly different.

In interviews in December of 2003, Jackson remarked that he "looked upon the ending" (Frodo's departure at the Grey Havens) as Tolkien's "metaphor" for "somebody's death."[48] And Jackson "tried to honor that. We tried to give it that sense of sadness. I feel it's extremely poignant that Frodo effectively is ultimately killed at the end of the story. I mean, he does ultimately die in the film; he can't live. And, yeah—it just makes it very sad."

The irony here is twofold: first, that Jackson is somehow saddened by the whole thing while his creative partners Boyens and Walsh find it rather hopeful. "I feel that something lifts from Frodo," said Walsh, "when he turns and looks back at the Hobbits."[49]

But the real kicker is that the stirring description of death that Boyens and Walsh provide for Gandalf, the line that also fueled their Oscar-winning song ("White shores—and beyond, a far green country under a swift sunrise") is taken from the very passage in which Tolkien describes Frodo's departure from the Grey Havens.[50]

Tolkien did very much believe that "There is a place called 'heaven' where the good here unfinished is completed,"[51] but the glimpse of the far green county and its swift sunrise was not death. It was the miraculous transportation from one physical place—Middle-earth—to another. Frodo was not passing from this world into death; he was sailing via the Straight Road on to Aman, a mystical but very physical place. It's doubtful that, for Tolkien, this was even a metaphor for purgatory, much less death. It does serve, however, as a useful metaphor for what Boyens and Walsh see in death, if not for what Jackson sees.

But would Tolkien have agreed, in accord with the implication of the cinema's Gandalf, that death is a positive thing in general? Not in Middle-earth. In "The Debate of Finrod and Andreth," the human plight is clearly articulated. Death is not a release, nor a "going home."[52] It's a grave evil, because—in Middle-earth, as in our world—the original divine design has been marred. Men are spiritually lost. For Tolkien, Middle-earth offered no release in death; the only honorable course was to live well and die well, and hope for nothing more. The architect of Middle-earth knew that the answer lay in the future, in our own world: it is faith, and faith in a Christian hope, a hope that does not disappoint—hope in the body and blood of the resurrected Jesus Christ.

As the Bible says, "There is a nice symmetry in this: Death initially came by a man, and resurrection from death came by a man. Everybody dies in Adam; everybody comes alive in Christ."[53]

❧ Jackson's Army of the Dead ☙

JUNE 2004

Probably the most startling—and most daring—change that Peter Jackson made to Tolkien's *The Return of the King* was the appearance of the Army of the Dead at the Battle of the Pelennor Fields. The moment at which Aragorn and company leap unexpectedly from the Black Ships and sweep the armies of Mordor before them comes straight from Tolkien, of course. In the book, though, the ships are not crewed by the Dead but by the Dúnedain of the North, subjects of Gondor from Lebennin, freed slaves, and Arwen's brothers Elladan and Elrohir. The "why" of Jackson's choice here is pretty straightforward: there's only so much screen time to go around, and bringing the Army of the Dead to Minas Tirith spares a great deal of exposition. But what are the detailed differences between Tolkien's and Jackson's narrative, and what intangibles (besides exposition and plotting) do audiences miss as a result of Jackson's audacious and successful truncation?

The Preparation, à la Jackson

In Jackson's version, the impetus for Aragorn to take the Paths of the Dead is much the same as it is in Tolkien: Minas Tirith is in imminent danger of assault, and much help must be brought in relief. The quickest path to bring help from the coastal regions of Gondor runs through the mountains, and only Aragorn has the requisite knowledge, mettle and destiny to brave that path. But Jackson elects to send Elrond as the lone emissary to prod Aragorn toward that road. Elrond, at Arwen's urging, has had the shards of Narsil reforged into Andúril, the Flame of the West, and he brings the sword to Aragorn at Dunharrow. Gandalf has previously hinted at the dark path that Aragorn will take to Minas Tirith, but it is Elrond, in Jackson's version of the story, who personally presses the Man Who Would Not Be King toward the portal of the road under the Ered Nimrais. In part, Jackson raises Elrond's profile at this stage of the story to demonstrate a change of heart toward Aragorn, and in part it's also a matter of plot simplification.

The Preparation, à la Tolkien

In the novel, Elrond still sends the same advice to Aragorn, but the message is sent via Elrond's sons Elladan and Elrohir, who have unexpectedly come south with a band of Aragorn's fellow Dúnedain. After joining Théoden and Aragorn on the road back to Helm's Deep from Isengard, the party encamps with them and shares the message that Elrond has sent with his sons: "Bid Aragorn remember the words of the seer, and the Paths of the Dead."[54] As is so often the case with Aragorn, prophets and seers have foretold long before the steps that he takes. "The crownless again shall be king,"[55] to be sure, and it is "need," as the seer Malbeth said in years long past, that drives the "heir" to summon the Dead to the Stone of Erech. For in Tolkien, Aragorn claims his right to the palantír of Orthanc and sees a fleet of ships in the south massing for an assault on Minas Tirith via Anduin. Aragorn must lead an army to head off the attack, for there is no other help to send—and he knows this before the party even sets out for Dunharrow from Helm's Deep.

And there's one more key element of preparation in Tolkien's version. Arwen, too, has sent a message for Aragorn: "The days now are short. Either our hope cometh, or all hope's end. Therefore I send thee what I have made for thee. Fare well,

Elfstone!"[56] Elladan and Elrohir bear her gift: a furled and cloaked banner on a tall staff. Aragorn already knows what it is, and knows what it is for—and bids his companions to bear it for him for just a while longer. In Tolkien, Arwen herself is as strong a player in Aragorn's decision as anyone is; and her very words remind him who he is, and for what he has spent long years in preparation. Jackson's Aragorn is unsettled by the prospect of the Paths of the Dead. Tolkien's Aragorn has long known how his path has been laid. Current events just make the need plain.

The Journey, à la Jackson

In Jackson's abbreviated version of the story, Aragorn and his two companions venture alone into the darkness beyond the Dark Door of the Dimholt, and afoot. Inside the mountain, Aragorn confronts the King of the Dead, and reminds him of the oath sworn to Isildur—the oath that was broken in the darkness of the past and that now may be made good by going to war against Mordor. The King of the Dead is convinced of Aragorn's right as Isildur's heir by the sword that Aragorn carries and by the force with which Aragorn wields it. Finally, at this point, Jackson's Aragorn asserts both his rights and his person.

From here, we are left to guess what happens to Aragorn and his ghostly army—and how they manage to arrive in timely fashion at Minas Tirith.

The Journey, à la Tolkien

In the novel, Aragorn travels not only with Legolas and Gimli, but also with the whole party of Dúnedain and the sons of Elrond—and their horses. Tolkien's Aragorn will lead his party on a hard four-day ride to battle, as slow travel afoot would leave Minas Tirith to a grisly fate. The passage of the Paths is brief (if evocative), and Aragorn's summons of the Dead is made not in the darkness of the mountain, but at night at the Stone of Erech in the Vale of Morthond. There he declares himself the heir of Isildur— "And with that, he bade Halbarad unfurl the great standard which he had brought; and behold! it was black, and if there was any device upon it, it was hidden in the darkness. Then there was silence, and not a whisper nor a sigh was heard again all the long night."[57] In Tolkien, it is not Andúril that awes the Dead, but the gift of Arwen.

As the Dead make their way through Lebennin, Aragorn asserts his command over them, and his authority awes his companions. They ride for days, pausing to rest but briefly, with Aragorn's endurance and concern for the fate of Minas Tirith driving them all.

The Battle

And in Tolkien, the Dead pay their debt at Pelargir, a port on Anduin where the Black Fleet of fifty-plus ships is massed. The men of Umbar and their allies from Harad are routed, and the Dúnedain take charge of the ships, now crewed by freed slaves and those men from the coastal regions of Gondor who manage to recover from their own fear of Aragorn's ghostly host. Aragorn releases the Dead from service, declaring their oath fulfilled, and they depart, finally at peace in death.

Jackson's film, of course, makes no attempt to explain how Aragorn commandeers the Black Fleet, and it is the Dead who disembark and turn the tide at the Pelennor rather than Men of Gondor.

What's Missing

I found the way in which the Dead swarm over the walls of Minas Tirith and Mordor's siege engines unfortunately reminiscent of cartoon termite attacks, accomplishing in mere seconds what would undoubtedly have taken Tolkien's Men hours. The dead who accompany Tolkien's "grey company" also become a ghastly green in Jackson's version—one which nonetheless manages to satisfyingly and effectively portray what Tolkien's spare description only suggests: the "grey tide"[58] of whispering hosts. To Jackson's credit, he also takes what might be the most objectionable element of Tolkien's story, and brings it to the forefront.

At the same time, it appears that Jackson's collapsed narrative manages to obscure the troubling implications of Tolkien's original version. Conservative critics have been oddly silent about ghosts warring on the side of "good"; yet liberal critics have also completely missed another observation: that Mordor's armies are themselves overcome by their own tactics— terror and darkness.

Was Tolkien a realist? To a certain extent, yes. He knew enough of the world, and of war, to know that the tools of "evil" often rebound onto themselves—that as one side ups the ante, the other side sees the bet (to extend the metaphor) and often raises. Escalation is a hallmark of war.

But Tolkien was also enough of an idealist to incorporate this fact into his narrative: that the treachery of Mordor's past (not merely tactical escalation) was its undoing in the present.

Still, there's a principle at work in this episode of Tolkien's novel that warrants closer examination. Is terror a tool that we should employ in the war *against* terror? The events at Abu Ghraib in Iraq suggest that for some the answer is "yes." For many the answer is "no." Where do we stand, as a nation? Are we satisfied with where we stand? Does the West really offer something better than terror, as we claim, or just more of the same?

> Do not repay evil with evil or insult with insult, but with blessing, because to this you were called so that you may inherit a blessing. For, "Whoever would love life and see good days must keep his tongue from evil and his lips from deceitful speech. He must turn from evil and do good; he must seek peace and pursue it..." Who is going to harm you if you are eager to do good? But even if you should suffer for what is right, you are blessed. "Do not fear what they fear; do not be frightened." ... It is better, if it is God's will, to suffer for doing good than for doing evil.[59]

ᔭ Our Own Private Tower of Cirith Ungol ᔰ

JULY 2004

If I were Thórr, I'd be pretty ticked. Someone has stolen my thunder! To be precise, two different guys have made off with my big rumble this month.

Way, way back last December, I started assembling the editorial plan for the year's *Lord of the Rings* features on Hollywood Jesus: twelve monthly guest features, twelve featured interviews, the make-it-up-as-we-go email-of-the-month, and twelve hard-hitting, incisive (and somewhat insightful) features in the vein of the pieces I'd done for the previous two years. Now, this was no great hardship and I didn't have too difficult a time developing an agenda that has, for the most part, kept a step or two ahead of HJ's very knowledgeable and loyal Tolkien fans.

And now, within the last two weeks, my pet topic for July— the propensity of evil to defeat itself in Tolkien's (and Jackson's) Middle-earth fantasy—has twice been soundly co-opted by readers over on HJ's *Rings* forum! These dudes are either stealing from my playbook, anticipating my next move like film-critique Robert E. Lees, or simply homing in on the same Tolkien wavelength as my own overactive brain.

This is no great tragedy, of course. But rather than go to the trouble of developing the whole thesis myself, I'll reprint the relevant sections of their posts, and then move on to examine some implications of their observations.

Sharp Minds, Good Points

First, David Marley, in a running conversation regarding the nature of evil in Middle-earth, makes the following observations:

> For the victory of good to have "moral significance," evil must be self-defeating. This cannot be the case if it has the power to overwhelm the weak and innocent, and force them to do its will. Evil corrupts through temptation, by offering individuals the power to do as they will—it exploits desire, convincing them that what they want is right. But the individual must have the choice to go along with that, or reject it.
>
> A moral victory requires that "good" wins because it is good, and "evil" loses because it is evil. If good wins because it happens to be stronger than evil, then the victory is of the strong over the weak, and it will be able to claim the title of "good" for itself merely because history is written by the winners.
>
> Hope, in the sense of "estel" (faith) as opposed to "amdir" (or simple optimism), requires that evil cannot ultimately win— that by its very nature it will bring about its own defeat. So the Manichean view must ultimately be false, because otherwise there will always remain the possibility that evil could in some way become powerful enough to overcome in the end, or at the very least, as I said, that it will lose only because it's not strong enough.
>
> Evil cannot "win" in the sense of having an overall victory, because it has no objective or "real" existence (according to Ainulindalë). It is an option—one can choose to behave in a particular way, which could be classed "evil"—but it has no existence in the sense that Ilúvatar has, or even that the things created by Ilúvatar have: evil does not possess the Secret Fire which alone guarantees true "existence." This is confirmed by its inability to create, and instead only mar what has been created.
>
> So, even if the forces that fight for good were defeated, evil's victory would not last, because (being unable to create, only

mar) it would turn on itself and so bring about its own destruction.[60]

Brian Overland, in an associated thread, then contributes the following:

> If you read the first part of *The Silmarillion*, I think you'll find the doctrine that evil is a kind of disharmony. It is clearly laid out there. To use other (but related) metaphors, you could characterize evil as a kind of spiritual sickness.
>
> In characterizing evil as disharmony of the soul (the sufferer is out of harmony both with Eru and his own best nature), Tolkien is not so different from Plato. Evil does not need to be punished so much as corrected and checked in this view, because the internal disharmony robs the sufferer from any real enjoyment of life regardless of evil's external victories. Certainly Sauron, simmering in his hatred and malice, was not relaxing and having a grand old party at the top of the Barad-dûr.
>
> As I've remarked to Greg several times, Sauron literally builds his own Hell, as does Morgoth before him. This, despite the fact that each originally lusted for something of beauty (the Silmarilli in the case of Morgoth, the power of the Elves in the case of Sauron).[61]

The arguments that these two students of Tolkien make are easily supported from the text of *The Lord of the Rings*, which is rife with instances of evil being defeated by its own devices: Saruman's mechanized despotism unwittingly bringing down the fury of the Ents, the treachery of Sauron's past rebounding on him through the Army of the Dead, Gollum's oath on the Ring bringing about not only his own demise but the destruction of the oath-binding Ring itself, and my own favorite example: the Orc-strife in the Tower of Cirith Ungol.

I'm hopeful, of course, that the Very Very Ultra Extra Special Extended Edition of *The Return of the King* will demonstrate to Jackson's cinematic audience exactly what happens in that tower. In the theatrical release, we see just the beginning of the spat between Shagrat and his comrades—and when Sam later comes to Frodo's rescue, it's entirely unclear why it's so easy for Sam to succeed in that insane task, and why only a handful of Orcs remain.

The Story Behind the Story

In the book there are even fewer Orcs left, and Snaga tumbles to his death (minus a hand, of course) rather than ending up skewered by a sneering (if passionately protective) Sam. Tolkien's narrative also provides a great deal more detail about the reasons for the slaughter in the Tower of Cirith Ungol.

In the first place, the tower is occupied by a mixed contingent of Orcs with divided loyalties; and while they are all dominated by Sauron's will, they still have differing agendas and—more importantly—are very focused on their own rights to life, obscene liberties, and the pursuit of greediness. Into this very unsettled and unwholesome mix comes Frodo's mithril shirt, which Gandalf noted was of greater value than the entire Shire. The Orcs, of course, well know its worth, and idle hands wreak great evil. The factions divide and conquer the garrison themselves, with Snaga left in the tower and the lone weasel Shagrat running off into the Morgai to report the carnage. Nothing is left for Sam to do but break the will of the Watchers at the gate. Then, finding the Orcs slain and while clutching at the Ring around his neck, Sam ascends the tower. His own stature is exaggerated by the presence of the Ring so that he appears "a great silent shape, cloaked in a grey shadow"[62]—a presence not unlike the Elf-warrior about which Shagrat's Orcs have speculated. In the penultimate room of the tower, Sam finds Snaga lashing Frodo with a whip and springs to his master's defense. Sting severs one of Snaga's arms, and the Orc then tumbles through an open hatch to his death.

Getting Beyond the Story

It's very easy to cite this scene as an example of how

Jackson has managed to twist Tolkien's intent, somehow making it a justification of preemptive "not if I stick you first"[63] international policies. It's also very easy to serve up a lesson on Tolkien's very Christian belief that evil is without a doubt its own worst enemy: "oft evil will shall evil mar,"[64] to quote Théoden's aphorism. And originally, those two points were all I intended to make.

David's and Brian's comments, though, have inspired me to take the discussion one step further. After all, if we're convinced that evil is its own undoing, can't we then argue (for example) that the United States really didn't need to go to war in Europe against Hitler? Germany wasn't attacking us, and the evil Nazi regime would have collapsed under its own weight at some point anyway, just like Reagan's lumbering Soviet bear. Right?

Yes, without a doubt. But there's still a cost of waiting for that to happen on its own. It's one thing to wait for a tower full of evil thugs to beat each other up—and I seriously doubt that there were any "innocent" victims at Cirith Ungol. When there are innocent bystanders to consider, however, the equation gets a little messier. How long do we pursue peaceful and diplomatic solutions to an international crisis, all the while knowing that thousands and thousands more innocent victims are dying while the talking and praying goes on? Sudan is a case in point, and I don't have an easy, canned, scriptural answer for that one, I'm afraid. But I am very sympathetic to the most-repeated refrain of Peter Jackson's films: What ultimately matters is what we do with the time that is given us.

I, for one, vow to forego further second-guessing of those who have to make such difficult decisions for our country. Instead, I intend: first, to pray for all those who have to make such decisions (God knows they can use such advocacy!); second, to use the time that is given me to halt injustice and suffering where I see it, without inducing further injustice and suffering in the process; and third, to do everything in my power to prevent divisiveness from bringing down the good that there is in this world. From what I've seen on C-SPAN lately, our own Congress is taking on a lot of the characteristics of the Tower of Cirith Ungol—much to our national shame and discredit. As human beings, we're better than that, and should demand better of ourselves and our leaders.

Have our politics turned us all into Orcs?

◈ Destroying Tolkien's *Rings* ◈

DECEMBER 2003

The Lord of the Rings Producer Barrie Osborne is no stranger to larger-than-life film productions. *Hearts of Darkness: A Filmmaker's Apocalypse* documents the creation of Francis Ford Coppola's celebrated *Apocalypse Now!* and also features Coppola's famous declaration at the Cannes press conference: "My movie is not about Vietnam... my movie *is* Vietnam!"[65] Michael Sragow, writing about Coppola at the website salon.com, notes that there was "something both lunatic and exhilarating" about Coppola's further explanation—"We had access to too much money, too much equipment, and little by little, we went insane."[66]

The Rising Action

Barrie Osborne was the Production Manager for *Apocalypse Now!* In interviews following press screenings of *The Return of the King* in L.A., Osborne downplayed any comparison between Jackson's films and Coppola's. But the comparisons are hard not to draw—not that New Line threw too much money or equipment at Tolkien's story, or that Jackson, et al., went crazy in the task; but in the same way that Coppola's film took on the character of its subject in the crucible of the production, so also did Jackson's cinematic trilogy take on the character of Frodo's struggle to destroy Sauron's Ring.

"The past seven years of my life has been consumed with writing, directing and producing *The Lord of the Rings* trilogy," Jackson wrote in publicity materials for *The Return of the King.* "It has been an exhausting journey, not unlike that of our fictional protagonists, Frodo and Sam; there has not been much sleep, no time for a normal life and there were days when we all wondered if we would make it to the end."[67]

But make it they did. And oddly enough, Jackson, Fran Walsh and Philippa Boyens—the three principal screenwriters for the *Rings* series—are just as perplexed, at this point in time, as Frodo and Sam at Mount Doom.

The Climax

If the last seven years' story arc—the production cycle for Jackson's *The Lord of the Rings*—is compared to the story arc of the movies themselves, the press screenings and international premieres of *Return* during the first week of December mark the climax of the story, just as the destruction of the Ring at Mount Doom marks the climax of Tolkien's story. And at Mount Doom, all Frodo and Sam really know is that the task has been more-or-less successfully completed; they are not really sure of their fate, nor sure of how history will remember their effort.

Jackson expresses some of this same feeling when he writes, "I am happy to let these films go off into the world and for them to become whatever this generation, or future generations, make of them. Whether my contribution is ultimately judged 'dainty or undainty,' it has now been made." But he is being somewhat disingenuous when he coyly concludes, "The trilogy is truly out of my hands now and in the hands of those for whom these films were made: the people who love these books and who have always loved film."[68]

The Denouement

The Return of the King, as we all know, is not really finished—nor is the trilogy finished, nor the story arc of Jackson's production concluded—until the postproduction and press tour is completed for the inevitable Special Extended Edition (and the full boxed set). There are even likely to be pick-ups and voice-overs for some actors. So what Jackson is really facing, and commenting on, is the denouement of his own story. Still to come for Jackson? His *own* Houses of Healing, his *own* Scouring of the Shire, his *own* Grey Havens. The difference is that Jackson knows these things lie before him—much as Frodo knows what lies before *him*, while Sam, Merry and Pippin somewhat blithely assume that Frodo will be around forever.

So what is Jackson's mood at this point? Not all that sunny. Take his opinion of the movie's ending as an example. While Walsh believes that Frodo's fate demonstrates a confidence that we "will endure in some form"[69]—that there's more to life than life, that Frodo himself transcends death—and concurs with the comfort of that vision, Jackson begs to differ. "It's extremely poignant that Frodo effectively is ultimately killed at the end of this film. I mean, he does ultimately *die* in the film. He can't live." He pauses to reflect a moment. "Yeah. It just makes [the conclusion] very sad."[70]

Fans who haven't seen the film need not be unduly alarmed by Jackson's comments; and those who have may be rightly befuddled. But if we remember that Jackson is still in the middle of his own story—and remember that he knows, like Frodo, that his own story is really still far from over—we can forgive him if he seems burdened by the sadness that weighs on him. He has carried the weight of his own Ring; and while Boyens and Walsh, like Sam, have helped carry him, they have not carried the Ring themselves, nor have they paid quite the personal price that Jackson has. It would be tempting to remark that Jackson still has his own cross to bear, if only he believed in such a thing.

So while Jackson's personal denouement sees cast and crew mostly go off on their merry way following the climax of the production's story arc—while Elijah Wood, Dominic Monaghan and Billy Boyd buy their home-away-from-work to enjoy together in New Zealand, while Sean Astin continues his own path as a director and father, while Orlando Bloom moves on to grand spectacles like *Pirates of the Caribbean 2* and *Troy*, and while Liv Tyler finds a new life in marriage—the tale is not yet over for Jackson. It's a good thing that he has found joy in the fellowship along the way, for there does not seem to be much joy left in the work that has been "prepared in advance"[71] for him to do.

"I have been lucky enough to work with some of the most talented cast and crew any filmmaker could wish for, anywhere in the world," he says. "Through the long years of production it was apparent that we all had one thing in common: a great and enduring love of the books, which in turn, resulted in an unfailing commitment to do our best work on these films."[72]

And with that, Jackson has come to his own Mount Doom, and has thrust his own burden into the flames: the weight of Tolkien's *Rings*.

Section Notes

[1] Sean Astin in The Return of the King Dir. Peter Jackson, Perf. Ian McKellen, Elijah Wood, Viggo Mortensen New Line Cinema 2003 DVD (New Line Home Video 2004).

[2] Billy Boyd in ibid.

[3] Dominic Monaghan in ibid.

[4] Billy Boyd in ibid.

[5] Ian McKellen in ibid.

[6] John Noble in ibid.

[7] J. R. R. Tolkien, Letters (Boston & New York: Houghton Mifflin Company, 2000), no. 5, to Geoffrey B. Smith, 1916.

[8] Elijah Wood in The Return of the King, op. cit.

[9] Annie Lennox in ibid.

[10] J. R. R. Tolkien, Letters, op. cit., no. 45, to Michael Tolkien, 1941.

[11] Ian McKellen in The Return of the King, op. cit.

[12] J. R. R. Tolkien, The Two Towers 2nd ed. (Boston: Houghton Mifflin Company, 1965), p. 203.

[13] J. R. R. Tolkien, ibid.

[14] J. R. R. Tolkien, Unfinished Tales Ed. Christopher Tolkien (Boston: Houghton Mifflin Company, 1980), p. 408.

[15] J. R. R. Tolkien, The Two Towers, op. cit., p. 200.

[16] Philippians 2:6, NIV.

[17] Philippa Boyens and Fran Walsh, Interview with Greg Wright et al. "A Coupla Kiwi Chicks Sitting Around Talking" (Hollywood Jesus 15 May 2004). 2 July 2004 [http://www.hollywoodjesus.com/lord_of_the_rings_interview_05.htm].

[18] "Every finite creature" wrote Tolkien, "must have some weakness: that is, some inadequacy to deal with some situations. It is not sinful when not willed, and when the creature does his best (even if it is not what should be done) as he sees it—with the conscious intent of serving Eru." J. R. R. Tolkien in footnote to essay on Melkor, Morgoth's Ring: The Later Silmarillion, Part One Ed. Christopher

Tolkien The History of Middle-earth Vol. 10 (Boston & New York: Houghton Mifflin Company, 1993), p. 392.

[19] J. R. R. Tolkien, The Two Towers, op. cit., p. 204.

[20] Romans 1:20.

[21] Ian McKellen in The Return of the King, op. cit.

[22] Ibid.

[23] Billy Boyd and Ian McKellen in The Return of the King, op. cit.

[24] Billy Boyd in The Fellowship of the Ring Dir. Peter Jackson, Perf. Ian McKellen, Elijah Wood, Viggo Mortensen New Line Cinema 2001 DVD (New Line Home Video 2002).

[25] Because Gandalf is the voice of wisdom in *The Lord of the Rings*, it's easy to take his words to Pippin about Frodo's quest as a "fool's hope" at face value—and even attribute the sentiment to Tolkien himself. However, the broader issue of hope in Middle-earth should also be taken into account, as well as Tolkien's commentary in the text. In the latter case, we must bear in mind that Gandalf is not speaking his own mind to Pippin. Instead, he is wryly commenting on what Denethor has only recently said to him. See J. R. R. Tolkien, The Return of the King, 2nd ed. (Boston: Houghton Mifflin Company, 1965), p. 87f.

[26] Billy Boyd in The Return of the King, op. cit.

[27] Ian McKellen in The Fellowship of the Ring, op. cit.

[28] J. R. R. Tolkien, The Two Towers, op. cit., p. 106.

[29] Romans 8:28, NIV.

[30] John 3:16.

[31] Ephesians 3:20, NIV.

[32] Booth Tarkington, Growth (New York: Doubleday, Page & Company, 1927), p. 1ff.

[33] J. R. R. Tolkien, The Two Towers, op. cit., p. 254f.

[34] Quotes in the following paragraphs regarding Sam's impressions of the oliphaunt are taken from J. R. R. Tolkien, The Two Towers, op. cit., p. 269f.

[35] J. R. R. Tolkien, The Return of the King, op. cit., p. 121.

[36] Descriptions of the Witch-king's steed in this paragraph are

taken from J. R. R. Tolkien, The Return of the King, op. cit., p. 115.

[37] Quotes in this paragraph regarding Lorien and Caras Galadon are taken from J. R. R. Tolkien, The Fellowship of the Ring 2nd ed. (Boston: Houghton Mifflin Company, 1965), pp. 357–369.

[38] The exchange between Pippin and Gandalf discussed in the following paragraphs is taken from Billy Boyd and Ian McKellen in The Return of the King, op. cit.

[39] Philippa Boyens and Fran Walsh, Interview with Greg Wright et al. op cit.

[40] Ibid.

[41] Sean Bean in The Fellowship of the Ring, op. cit.

[42] Ibid.

[43] Cate Blanchett in The Fellowship of the Ring Special Extended Edition Dir. Peter Jackson, Perf. Ian McKellen, Elijah Wood, Viggo Mortensen New Line Cinema 2002 DVD (New Line Home Video 2002).

[44] Cate Blanchett in The Fellowship of the Ring, op. cit.

[45] The exchange between Boromir and Aragorn in the following paragraphs is taken from Sean Bean and Viggo Mortensen in The Fellowship of the Ring, op. cit.

[46] Peter Jackson, Interview with Jeffrey Overstreet et al. (Looking Closer 2003). 2 July 2004 [http://promontoryartists/lookingcloser/movie%20reviews/Q-Z/returnoftheking-jackson.htm].

[47] The Return of the King Trailer New Line Cinema 2003 (2 July 2004 [http://www.lordoftherings.net/trailer_rotk_trailer_small.html]).

[48] Jackson's quotes regarding death in the following paragraphs are taken from Peter Jackson, Interview with Greg Wright et al. "The Horse's Mouth" (Hollywood Jesus 15 April 2004). 2 July 2004 [http://www.hollywoodjesus.com/lord_of_the_rings_interview_05.htm].

[49] Philippa Boyens and Fran Walsh, Interview with Greg Wright et al. op cit.

[50] J. R. R. Tolkien, The Return of the King, op. cit., p. 310.

[51] J. R. R. Tolkien, Letters, op. cit., no. 45, to Michael Tolkien, 1941.

[52] J. R. R. Tolkien, Morgoth's Ring, op. cit., p. 317.

[53] I Corinthians 15:21–22, *The Message.*

[54] J. R. R. Tolkien, The Return of the King, op. cit., p. 54.

[55] J. R. R. Tolkien, The Fellowship of the Ring, op. cit., p. 182

[56] J. R. R. Tolkien, The Return of the King, op. cit., p. 48.

[57] Ibid., p. 63.

[58] Ibid., p. 152.

[59] I Peter 3:9–17, NIV.

[60] This passage was originally excerpted from post number 762 (06/30/04) on the Hollywood Jesus *The Lord of the Rings* Forum. See [http://forums.gospelcom.net/view/hollywoodjesus/lord_of_the_rings/].

[61] This passage was originally excerpted from post number 780 (07/07/04) on the Hollywood Jesus *The Lord of the Rings* Forum. See [http://forums.gospelcom.net/view/hollywoodjesus/lord_of_the_rings/].

[62] J. R. R. Tolkien, The Return of the King, op. cit., p. 180.

[63] Sean Astin in The Return of the King, op. cit.

[64] J. R. R. Tolkien, The Two Towers, op. cit., p. 200.

[65] Francis Ford Coppola in Hearts of Darkness, A Filmmaker's Apocalypse Dir. Fax Bahr, with George Hickenlooper Perf. Francis Ford Coppola, Martin Sheen, Dennis Hopper American Zoetrope 1991 Videocassette (Paramount Pictures, 1992).

[66] Michael Sragow, "Francis Ford Coppola" (salon.com 19 Oct. 1999). 2 July 2004 [http://archive.salon.com/people/bc/1999/10/19 /coppola/index.html].

[67] Peter Jackson in The Return of the King Digital Press Kit Insert, New Line Cinema, 2003.

[68] Ibid.

[69] Philippa Boyens and Fran Walsh, Interview with Greg Wright et al. op. cit.

[70] Peter Jackson, Interview with Greg Wright et al. op. cit.

[71] Ephesians 2:10, NIV.

[72] Peter Jackson in The Return of the King Digital Press Kit Insert, op. cit.

The Spirit of Tolkien

ঙ Grilling Jackson, Boyens and Walsh ঙ

LECTURE, MARCH 2004

More than once, Peter Jackson has rather famously remarked, "We made a real decision at the beginning that we weren't going to introduce any new themes of our own into *The Lord of the Rings*. We wanted to make a film that was based on what Tolkien was passionate about."[1]

Talking directly with Jackson, Philippa Boyens and Fran Walsh yields tremendous insight into what they feel Tolkien was passionate about. If Jackson, Boyens and Walsh are the cinematic guardians of the "Spirit of Tolkien," as expressed in *The Lord of the Rings*, what is their take on that spirit?

Differing Perspectives on Death

During the Academy Awards telecast in February 2004, and the Golden Globe awards, Fran Walsh made rather cryptic references to Cameron Duncan. In interviews conducted in tandem with Philippa Boyens in December 2003, she said:

> It's a curious thing we've been going through this year. We lost a young and dear friend, a young boy, to cancer, and watching him face his mortality, at seventeen, and watching him come to terms with the knowledge of his impending death, and how he and his family dealt with that. We were

169

part of that as we finished this film, and I felt very strongly that, in the film, death—when Frodo crosses over—that it's not a negative thing. And I felt that for Cameron, too. Because he was so ravaged and ill, that it, you know, it freed him. And it released him. And I feel that in the film, too. I feel that something lifts from Frodo, when he turns and looks back at the Hobbits... And I really liked that the film shows it in that way. Because often it's such a thing of fear, and dread, you know—that in films it's portrayed in that way, and yet there is another way to view it. And we saw it play out, you know, in our own lives with Cameron. And to see it in the film, too, I really liked that about the movie.[2]

Boyens added, "It's definitely deliberately done. But what I loved is that Ian McKellen made you feel good about it."[3]

So obviously, death is one of the central issues in *The Lord of the Rings*. And Boyens and Walsh are certainly right that death is one of the things that Tolkien is writing about. It is part of that "spirit of Tolkien." But it's perhaps troublesome to consider Jackson's assertion that they didn't want to bring their own baggage to *The Lord of the Rings*, because even in connection to the subject of death Jackson doesn't agree with Boyens or Fran Walsh, the mother of his children. If they can't agree among themselves about such key issues, how can they agree about how to interpret and present Tolkien's ideas?

Boyens and Walsh, though, tend to play off each other like peas in a pod in interviews. They will complete each other's ideas and thoughts, and appear completely in sync with the other's ideas and attitudes. Yet while the two of them can be very encouraged by the depiction of death in *The Return of the King*, Peter Jackson has very different things to say:

We looked upon the ending, really, as being a metaphor for Frodo passing the shore, that he—that you were 'fare-welling' somebody who was, who seemed to be dying. I mean, he was going to this blessed land, and he—we do certainly feel that Tolkien regarded that as being a visualization of somebody's death. He said, well, you get on a ship and you sail out into the harbor, and farewell them into this light—but it's fairly obvious what Tolkien was really referring to. And we tried to honor that—we tried to give it that sense of sadness. I feel it's extremely poignant that Frodo is ultimately effectively killed at the end of the story; I mean, he does ultimately die in the film; he can't live. And, yeah—it just makes it very sad.[4]

That's a very surprising comment from Peter Jackson. I doubt most audience members come away from *The Return of the King* thinking that Frodo is dead, and that his is some incredibly sad fate. So where does this come from? How does Peter Jackson, as the maker of the film, view such a central element so differently from Boyens and Walsh? Let's turn to Tolkien for some insight.

Tolkien, Death and Middle-earth

In "The Debate of Finrod and Andreth," Tolkien wrote extensively about the issue of the mortality of Men versus the relative immortality of Elves, and the nature of death in Middle-earth.[5] Finrod, in that tale, is surprised at the pessimistic attitude of Men toward death. He says to Andreth, "'death' would... have sounded... as a release, or return, nay! as going home." And the reason that Finrod thinks this is because he doesn't understand Men and their attitude about death—that Men fear death, and that it's generally perceived to be a bad thing.

Interestingly, the passage that Boyens and Walsh put into Gandalf's mouth in *The Return of the King* regarding death is lifted from the very end of *The Lord of the Rings*, the next to the last page of *The Return of the King*.

> The ship went out into the High Sea and passed on into the West, until at last on a night of rain Frodo smelled a sweet fragrance on the air and heard the sound of singing that came over the water. And then it seemed to him that as in his dream in the house of Bombadil, the grey rain-curtain turned all to silver glass and was rolled back, and he beheld white shores and beyond them a far green country under a swift

sunrise.[6]

Those words have now even made their way into the Oscar-winning song penned by Fran Walsh and Howard Shore, "Into the West." But when Tolkien wrote those words, he was not describing death. He was describing a concrete, physical place outside the confines of Middle-earth. He was writing about Valinor, the Undying Lands. And it's not the experience of death, it's a real place to which Frodo goes. Frodo goes on to live in Valinor until he comes to his natural death many years later; and then his fate is as other Men and Hobbits. Sailing off in the Grey Ships does not change the nature or experience of death for him.

This is an element of the "Spirit of Tolkien" that Jackson, Boyens and Walsh just don't seem to understand. Now, is the portrayal of death in *The Return of the King* negative? No. In fact, it might even be overly hopeful. But their portrayal of death, when examined alongside some other aspects of issues in Tolkien, should give us some cause for concern about how deeply Jackson and his crew really understood Tolkien before undertaking the films.

Tolkien, Evil and the Fall of Man

In Tolkien's letters, he wrote about what he saw as the core issue of storytelling in general, and certainly, by extension, of *The Lord of the Rings*. He wrote, "There cannot be any 'story' without a Fall—all stories are ultimately about the Fall."[7] What does he mean when he writes that? Well, as a Roman Catholic, he has a very specific understanding of "the Fall" and of the fallenness of Man. So, whether we like it or not, if we want to understand the spirit of Tolkien, we have to delve to some extent into issues of Christian, and specifically Roman Catholic, beliefs.

In Christianity, the Fall of Man is tied to the story of Eden. Every story that we tell, Tolkien believed, is some variation of the story of the Garden of Eden, in which Adam and Eve defied God's words and will, and then were cast out of Eden. This fallenness, in

Roman Catholic belief, affects the entire world around us. Individuals, the nature of good and evil in the world, the very nature of the world, creation itself, the fate of Man—everything is tied up with this notion of the Fall.

In Tolkien's mythology, this comes out explicitly in a couple of places. In *The Silmarillion* and related writings, the Fall happens with both Men and with Elves at different times. In Tolkien's unwritten history of Men, at some point they are corrupted by Melkor and their created, perfect nature is forever tainted and broken. Eru did not create Men to die, but to be deathless, physically and spiritually. But that intent is spoiled because, as in the Garden of Eden, Man listens to a fallen angel rather than to God. And the fear of death originates not in the created, given nature of Men, but in their Fall. As Paul writes in the Bible, speaking of Adam, "through one man sin entered the world."[8]

Later, when the Númenóreans decide to follow Sauron and assault Valinor, the gods destroy Númenor with an earthquake and a tsunami, and Aragorn's ancestors are cast ashore in Middle-earth. For Tolkien, this was the "Second Fall"[9] of Man: once again, disregarding the beneficence of the Valar and turning aside to follow the lies of the deceiver. Once more we find the consequence of rebelliousness.

And we see this with the Elves, too. The Elves are not perfect. They also revolt against the Valar and are exiled from Valinor to Middle-earth. Galadriel is one of the leaders of the rebellion, along with the sons of Fëanor. They do not submit themselves to the will of the gods and are punished for their willfulness.

These are the issues about which Tolkien writes, speaking of the glory and "heart-wracking sense of the vanished past."[10] Tolkien does not merely recommend the "good old days." He points out that, if we go back far enough, we get beyond the Fall of Man and back to an existence perfected in God's will. And this is a very Christian understanding of the nature of the world.

Tied up with this is the problem of evil. Because of the fallen nature of the world, evil will always exist, within us and external to us. Evil is not just a man-centered thing, nor is it just outside ourselves, oppressing us. So Tolkien can write, "It is possible for the good, even the saintly, to be subjected to a power of evil which is too great for them to overcome—in themselves."[11]

Evil and Jackson's Middle-earth

But when we ask Peter Jackson about evil, he says, "I don't know whether evil exists. You see stuff happening around the world and you believe it probably does. I think that human beings are not capable... I think that evil exists within people. I don't know whether it exists as a force outside of humanity."[12] He goes on to say,

> The whole thing with *The Lord of the Rings* is that [the Age of Elves] is now past and men are going to inherit this world... He knew that Aragorn inheriting the world and mankind taking over was only going to lead to World War One eventually, because he imagined this book as happening six thousand years ago. He certainly wasn't writing with a degree of triumph that mankind is now in charge. He felt that we are flawed and that we don't deserve to be in charge of the world.[13]

While Jackson rightly perceives Tolkien's conviction of Man's brokenness, he exempts the Elves. "One of the things that's in Tolkien's book too is this feeling that the Elves are this perfect race. They're intelligent, they're sophisticated... They're spiritual. If you have the Elves in charge of the world, there will be no wars, there will be no hatred."[14] Here he badly misses the mark. The world would be a poor place indeed if the sons of Fëanor, for example, were in charge.

There is indeed evil in Middle-earth—and it does corrupt Elves, too. But does the "the Fall" find its way into the movies? Perhaps. Boyens sees pride as one expression of fallenness. "I think that's critical to good drama—you know," she says. "Hubris is (and all of it is) what makes a great story. Certainly with a lot of the characters, yes. Absolutely. I think Saruman falls. I mean, a lot of the characters. And that's actually the way in which the Ring consciously works as a source of evil is to—"

And here, Walsh picks up the thought without missing a beat. "—deny free will. And that seems to be the tenet underlying the story—is his Catholicism, which is sort of at the heart, I think, of the things, hopefully, in the film and in the book. And in the end, I think if there's anything to be taken from the film, it's that—it's about faith. That there is—it's also about death, and deathlessness—it's about the knowledge that you will endure in some form." Boyens continues,

> And you don't fall if you have faith. That's the other thing, I think, in this. There is no fall with faith. In terms of holding—well, in terms of, say, some of the things in this film, and, I believe, in the books—in terms of holding true to yourself, and in terms of holding true to a sense of goodness and decency, in terms of holding true to your fellowship with your fellow man, all of those things. You know, seeking and striving for that sense of decency, I think, and goodness. But also understanding that we're flawed, you know, because that's what he said. You know, that a note of discord was struck in the creation of the world, and all that kind of stuff. We—you know, you can't make it overt within the story, such as it is, but it certainly informed what we were doing, and informed (to go back to the beginning of what we were discussing) what we talked about with the actors when they first got off the plane. It began to inform what they were doing, as well. So whether or not it's ever explicit, it's certainly underneath there.[15]

It's heartening, of course, to see Boyens and Walsh explicitly acknowledging Tolkien's Catholicism. They do have an understanding that humans aren't perfect, and that we do fail. We're inherently flawed, yes. But the two writers have very little grasp of the Roman Catholic understanding of fallenness. A Catholic would not say "there is no fall with faith." A Catholic believes that we can be saved by Grace, through faith, in spite of our fallenness. But faith does not prevent us from falling. It restores a right relationship with God through the atonement, or substitutionary sacrifice, made available through the death of Jesus. That's quite a different thing, and a better. It makes moral failure less a crisis of faith than an opportunity for grace.

Catholic Theology and Middle-earth

So I asked Philippa Boyens and Fran Walsh specifically about the extent to which they pursued the Catholic issues in *The Lord of the Rings*. After all, I'm no expert in Catholic theology myself and need to consult experts from time to time. Did they? Walsh replied,

> I don't know to what extent [Tolkien] consciously sort of put it into the story. Just as he denied that it was ever an allegory for World War II and all that—although clearly his war experiences very much inform the books—equally so, his personal beliefs inform the books and his philosophies. And I think that—but not so that he's driving an agenda. I don't believe that. But there are certainly, you know, parallels that you can draw between Frodo's journey and that of, you know, the Christ story—you can, because it's about sacrifice, and it's about... I think at the end of the movie, and I feel it very strongly, that he transitions to another place. Which is—that's another way of looking at faith in the story—that he doesn't die, and that Gandalf is his guide (in that he's an angelic character). So I found it quite comforting, in a strange way, and I don't think it's necessarily, in that way, specifically Catholic.[16]

It's certainly true that there are broader principles at work in *The Lord of the Rings*. Tolkien studied the full range of pagan mythology and incorporated many of its elements into his work, but I imagine that Tolkien would have begged to differ with Walsh's contention that his story's objectives were not specifically Catholic. And it's not too hard to confirm that suspicion, either.

Tolkien explicitly said, *"The Lord of the Rings* is of course a fundamentally religious and Catholic work... The religious element is absorbed into the story and the symbolism... unconsciously at first, but consciously in the revision."[17]

So if we can take Tolkien's word on this issue, rather than Walsh's, what does that really mean for Tolkien? Not what that means for me, or for Walsh, or Jackson or Boyens—but for Tolkien himself? We can get a handle on the true spirit of Tolkien, and how it informs *The Lord of the Rings,* by examining three key teachings of the Roman Catholic Church, and comparing those teachings with what Jackson and company have to say.

Christian Humanism

The first of these teachings is the idea of *Christian humanism,* which is a tempered belief in the worth of the individual—"a consistent theme in the teaching of Jesus... The Christian humanist values culture but confesses that man is fully developed only as he comes into a right relationship with Christ."[18] In philosophy, this idea is distinct from the more general *humanism* which sprang from the Enlightenment. When the West rediscovered the ancient philosophies of Greece, and of the ancient Roman Catholic Church, what resulted was an affirmation of the value of human life, the value of human reason, and the value of the individual as an individual. Humanism, then, is "an educational and philosophical outlook that emphasizes the personal worth of the individual and the central importance of human values as opposed to religious belief... Human beings can satisfy religious needs from within, discarding the concept of God as inconsistent with advanced thought and human freedom."[19]

Christian humanism, then, while it embraces the value of the individual, does so not for the sake of the individual but for the sake of God and the importance that God places on the individual; and this, of course, is not opposed to religious belief, but compatible with (and grounded in) religious belief. The difference between Christian humanism and general humanism is quite marked.

Do Boyens and Walsh understand that difference? Boyens asserts that, "If anything, Tolkien's faith informs the third book… It's certainly faith that the enduring goodness of men and in men will prevail. Faith that even those who leave us too soon or who are lost in war or who die young—and Frodo certainly represents all of those—they go to another place, they don't just fall into nothingness. They transition to somewhere else. Faith that we can all be better than we are." She continues by saying that *The Lord of the Rings* is

> about the enduring power of goodness, that we feel it in ourselves when we perceive it in others in small acts every day in other people. And that gives you reason to hope that it has significance for all of us as a race, as mankind, that we're evolving and getting better rather than becoming less, diminishing ourselves through hatred and cruelty. We need to believe that. We need to have a sense of preparation.[20]

Do we need to diminish hatred and cruelty in the world? Absolutely. Is Boyens' understanding of the value of humanism valid? Yes. But Boyens believes, unlike Christian humanists, that the solution is within us rather than in a right relationship with Christ.

Natural Law

A second key teaching of the Roman Catholic Church is the idea of *Natural Law*. Thomas Aquinas argued that there is first Eternal Law, principles which God ordained and which are immutable because they come from God. God also, then, reveals Himself in nature, and from human observation of the world we can derive Natural Law: a glimpse of Eternal Law that is revealed about God, by God, through His creation. Natural Law does not reveal God Himself, as would the ideal of Eternal Law. Rather, it is a manifestation of God that is perceptible to human beings because we are ourselves natural and participate in Natural Law.

So even if God did not reveal Himself to us through Scripture or through His prophets—which the Roman Catholic Church asserts that He has—humans would still innately sense God, and know of Him, through our apprehension of Natural Law. As Descartes asserted, "I think, therefore I am." For Descartes, this was an affirmation of God, not merely a celebration of reason.

Hand in hand with Natural Law operates *Free Will*, the idea that we, as individuals and independent moral agents, have the choice to do what we will—again, as in Eden when Man chose not to follow God. Even though God is in control and He ordains events, that fact does not remove personal responsibility from the equation. We act, we make choices, and there are consequences. This is constantly apparent in *The Lord of the Rings*. Boromir has the choice whether to take the Ring from Frodo, just as Aragorn does—and he makes a different choice than does Aragorn. Frodo has the choice whether to take the Ring to Minas Tirith, or whether to take the Ring to Mordor. Those are choices, and that's the exercise of Free Will. But at the same time, there are other forces operating in conjunction with Free Will. There is real good and tangible evil, both exerting themselves to influence the exercise of Free Will, and there is Providence guiding all things, turning even seeming evil to good. A Catholic theologian explains, "Like all the rest of creation, man is destined by God to an end, and receives from Him a direction towards this end. This ordination is of a character in harmony with his free intelligent nature. In virtue of his intelligence and free will, man is master of his conduct."[21] This is Natural Law at work.

By contrast, Peter Jackson says that the Ring "symbolizes a loss of free will, really...What the Ring seems to be offering to people is a sense of power, but it invites you to use your power for good. If you're a good person, you think that you can use the Ring for good."[22] The Ring, certainly, exercises influence over individuals—but Tolkien would explain that such evil does not gain any more control over individuals than they want to cede to it, or more influence than God providentially grants. Free will is not co-opted. Jackson, however, is not convinced. "Tolkien," he says, very much asserts through his writing that "the value at stake is your free will and your freedom." Further, Jackson says, the novel does not merely depict a physical bondage in which "these Orcs are going to invade and make you prisoner and enslave you, which is one aspect of it," but that "the Ring is like the metaphor for enslavement."[23]

Again, for Jackson, evil is synonymous with the loss of individual freedom. He implies that temptation does not originate in our own evil desires—as the Bible asserts[24]—but in forces outside of us.

Tolkien and Peter Jackson agree, however, that humanity is not going to lift itself out of this mess. Tolkien, in fact, sees one of the functions of his fiction as a means of holding up a mirror to humanity and letting us see ourselves as we really are, in "scorn and pity."[25] Einstein observed that the same level of thinking that gets us into a scrape is not going to be sufficient to get us out of it. We have problems in this world because we're human; and merely being human is not a solution, if you believe Roman Catholic theology—if you believe what Tolkien believed. So what *is* the solution?

Salvation History

This question leads to a third teaching of the Roman Catholic Church, the concept of *Salvation History*: the active movement of God's hand throughout history to restore Man to a right relationship to Himself. What's behind this idea is the doctrine of Providence, the assertion that God is in control of everything. "The mechanism," I've noted elsewhere, "is a Christian humanist exercise of the rational free will of every created being, each acting in accordance with inescapable natural law, to fulfill the larger purposes of God's grand designs, even when we freely and sinfully act contrary to natural law."[26]

Providence, of course, is clearly seen in *The Lord of the Rings*, as Boyens says:

180

One of the things Tolkien understood because he was a humanist... is that we are all frail, and we have the ability within us to fail at any stage. Faith requires us to believe in a higher power. Gandalf, very early on in the book, says "The Ring came to Bilbo and in that moment something else was at work." Not the design of its maker—this evil power—but some other power was at work. So it's whether you believe in that or not, whether you choose to believe in that or not. Actually that was the combination. Frodo dragged himself to that point and failed. And another power intervened. And he ultimately surrenders to that power at the end of this movie, which is one of the most beautiful moments in this movie... when Frodo turns and he smiles. That is his redemption.[27]

Philippa Boyens does see the hand of God playing into things. We all see at the end, when Gollum rips the Ring from Frodo's hand and then tumbles into the Crack of Doom, that there is something controlling events: that Gollum was necessary all along the way—even though he might be perceived as an evil force—in the playing out of the grand scheme of things. It takes the good *and* the evil for God—or, in the case of Middle-earth, Eru—to bring about His will to make things happen. So that's hopeful. But Boyens still attributes this hopefulness to Tolkien's humanism, not to his faith.

What Happens at Mount Doom?

In interviews with the cast and crew, over a dozen different individuals were asked the question, "So, who destroyed the Ring?" It seems a simple question, but so many different answers were given it's hard to believe that the issue was ever discussed by the cast and crew. Peter Jackson's take was that Frodo and Gollum "do accidentally fall in, while the two of them are trying to fight for ownership of the Ring. ... The pity of Bilbo is all about placing Gollum at the Crack of Doom. Without the pity, he would have been dead before they got to the Crack of Doom."[28] Now, Jackson's use of the term "accident" here raises some warning flags—because those who believe in Providence don't take much stock in "accidental" occurrences. Individuals exercise their free will in accordance with God's grand designs, which is personal responsibility and Providence—there's no luck involved, and it's not blind determinism either. So I pressed Jackson on this point, and asked if Gollum's tumble into the Crack of Doom really might not be considered providential. He merely looked at me in a rather amused fashion, and would only say, "Yes."[29] He elected not to elaborate when I waited for further clarification, and merely repeated his single-word response.

All of this is rather disconcerting because Boyens and Walsh represent themselves matter-of-factly as the ones who were the keepers of Tolkien's vision. "One of the things that most of the actors needed," says Boyens, "was to be brought into this world. Because, for a lot of them, they weren't all huge Tolkien fans, and that was part of the process, was—they'd come, get off the plane, and the first thing, it was like Tolkien 101. It was what we did."[30]

Boyens, Walsh and Tolkien 101

Tolkien boot camp for everyone who came onto the project—the actors, the crew, everybody. Boyens and Walsh instructed them in the "Spirit of Tolkien" so they could all be on the same page. Yet if the two of them don't really have a grasp of the foundational issues behind Tolkien's fiction, how can they instruct others? And in talking to the various people involved, I found very little consistent opinion about what the "Spirit of Tolkien" actually was. In fact, Ian McKellen was often cited as the "go-to" guy when it came to questions about the text, yet Christopher Lee openly considered himself the guardian of the text. So who were, in fact, the guardians? From my own point of view—and I was frankly very surprised by the discovery—Liv Tyler actually came off as the one who was in reality the most well-versed in Tolkien's work. And this was ironic since her character is the one most badly mangled in the films as released. Perhaps it's an odd form of divine justice.

The Spirit of Tolkien

I was certainly surprised at Boyens and Walsh failing to consult experts on Catholicism, but I was dumbfounded to discover that Howard Shore first heard about the Music of the Ainur from members of the religious press in December of 2002.[31] I was then utterly flabbergasted that, when I asked Peter Jackson if Tolkien's theory of "eucatastrophe" had been broached in story conferences, he replied, "No, what's it mean?"[32]

In moments such as these, my own Tolkien territorialism and self-righteousness kicked in. I actually felt like asking no further questions because I felt that Jackson, Boyens and Walsh simply hadn't done their homework. They wanted to claim, I thought indignantly, that they had preserved the spirit of Tolkien, yet without really having studied Tolkien. Sure, they read *The Lord of the Rings*, and liked it a lot—but did they really understand what's behind *The Lord of the Rings*? It seemed to me that they did not. As readers at Hollywood Jesus know, of course, the shoe has often enough been on the other foot and I should not have been so quick to cast my own Third-age stones.

And after all, have Jackson's shortcomings been so disastrous? In the ultimate scheme of things, no, though fans (and critics) may be disappointed to find out that the filmmakers aren't quite as "serious" about Tolkien's fiction as some of us think that we ourselves are.

There is an intangible upside to the involvement of Jackson, Boyens and Walsh, though, beyond the obvious fact that they succeeded in making some terrific films. These are good people, who have good, solid moral and spiritual values, and who believe in the value of human life. We could have done a lot worse than Jackson (and company) as the guiding force behind the cinema's *The Lord of the Rings*.

Boyens on Faith in *The Lord of the Rings*

"It's the higher power, when you ask what it is—that's what it is. That's what faith is. Ultimately a belief in a higher power, and another plane on which you can exist. And that spans a lot of belief systems, which Tolkien himself knew because he was drawing on a wider mythology and his own love of that wider mythology. And he was seeking—what I love about it is it's still so English—it's adorably English—the comfort, like you say, it's comfort. It's about the fireside, and the hearth and the home, and the friendship and that—all those things, and decent thinking and goodness, that he found in the trenches in World War I: stoicism, and that's Sam."[33]

Jackson on Hope in *The Lord of the Rings*

"I agree that hope is there. At least, I *hope* hope is there! It must be about hope. I don't think the alternative is particularly attractive. There has to be some degree of hope."[34]

Walsh on Charity in *The Lord of the Rings*

"He took that from his own war experience and from his own profound Christian beliefs. Those ideas in the book—we attempted as much as we could to invest them in the film. The values in them, they give you a sense of hope, that it isn't chaos, that it isn't arbitrary, that it isn't without a point. I love storytelling for those reasons, because so many things fall away as we charge forward into this new century. There's so much cynicism and such a lack of ritual and a belief system to govern anything. I like stories for that because they still offer it."[35]

And the greatest of these is still charity, as attested in the Greatest Story Ever Told.

Section Notes

[1] Peter Jackson, Interview with Jeffrey Overstreet et al. (Looking Closer 2003). 2 July 2004 [http://promontoryartists/lookingcloser/mo vie%20reviews/Q-Z/returnoftheking-jackson.htm].

[2] Philippa Boyens and Fran Walsh, Interview with Greg Wright et al. "A Coupla Kiwi Chicks Sitting Around Talking" (Hollywood Jesus 15 May 2004). 2 July 2004 [http://www.hollywoodjesus.com /lord_of_the_rings_interview_05.htm].

[3] Ibid.

[4] Peter Jackson, Interview with Greg Wright et al. "The Horse's Mouth" (Hollywood Jesus 15 April 2004). 2 July 2004 [http://www. hollywoodjesus.com/lord_of_the_rings_interview_05.htm].

[5] For the several references in this section to "The Debate of Finrod and Andreth," see J. R. R. Tolkien, Morgoth's Ring: The Later Silmarillion, Part One Ed. Christopher Tolkien The History of Middle-earth Vol. 10 (Boston & New York: Houghton Mifflin Company, 1993), p. 304ff.

[6] J. R. R. Tolkien, The Return of the King 2nd ed. (Boston: Houghton Mifflin Company, 1965), p. 310.

[7] J. R. R. Tolkien, Letters (Boston & New York: Houghton Mifflin Company, 2000), no. 131, to Milton Waldman, 1951.

[8] Romans 5:12, NASB.

[9] J. R. R. Tolkien, Letters, op. cit., no. 131, to Milton Waldman, 1951.

[10] Ibid., no. 96, to Christopher Tolkien, 1945.

[11] Ibid., no. 192, to Amy Ronald, 1956.

[12] Peter Jackson, Interview with Jeffrey Overstreet et al. op. cit.

[13] Ibid.

[14] Ibid.

[15] Philippa Boyens and Fran Walsh, Interview with Greg Wright et al. op. cit.

[16] Ibid.

[17] J. R. R. Tolkien, Letters, op. cit., no. 142, to Robert Murray, 1953.

[18] R. G. Clouse, "Christian Humanism" (Believe Religious Information Source) Oct. 21, 2002 [mb-soft.com/believe/txn/chrishum .htm].

[19] Benjamin G. Kohl, "Humanism" (Believe Religious Information Source). Oct. 21, 2002 [mbsoft.com/believe/txn/chrishum.htm].

[20] Philippa Boyens and Fran Walsh Interview with Jeffrey Overstreet et al. (Looking Closer 2003). 2 July 2004 [http://promontoryartists/lookingcloser/movie%20reviews/Q-Z/return oftheking-franphilippa.htm].

[21] James J. Fox, "Natural Law" The Catholic Encyclopedia Volume 9 (New York: Robert Appleton Company, 1910, Online Edition: Kevin Knight, 1999). Oct. 21, 2002 [www.newadvent .org/cathen/09076a.htm].

[22] Peter Jackson, Interview with Greg Wright et al. op. cit.

[23] Peter Jackson, Unpublished Interview with David Bruce et al. Audio CD (New Line Cinema December 2004).

[24] See James 1:13–15.

[25] J. R. R. Tolkien, The Tolkien Reader (New York: Ballantine Books, 1966) p. 52.

[26] Greg Wright, Tolkien In Perspective (Sisters, Oregon: VMI, 203) p. 165.

[27] Philippa Boyens and Fran Walsh, Interview with Jeffrey Overstreet et al. op. cit.

[28] Peter Jackson, Interview with Greg Wright et al. op. cit.

[29] Ibid.

[30] Philippa Boyens and Fran Walsh, Interview with Greg Wright et al. op. cit.

[31] Howard Shore, Unpublished Interview with David Bruce et al. Audio CD (New Line Cinema December 2004).

[32] Peter Jackson, Interview with Greg Wright et al. op. cit.

[33] Philippa Boyens and Fran Walsh, Interview with Greg Wright et al. op. cit.

[34] Peter Jackson, Interview with Jeffrey Overstreet et al. op. cit.

[35] Philippa Boyens and Fran Walsh Interview with Jeffrey Overstreet et al. op. cit.

Bibliography

Astin, Sean. Interview with Greg Wright, et al. "The Hobbit Next Door." Hollywood Jesus 15 June 2004. 2 July 2004 [http://www.hollywoodjesus.com/lord_of_the_rings_intervie w_06.htm].

Boyens, Philippa and Fran Walsh. Interview with Greg Wright, et al. "A Coupla Kiwi Chicks Sitting Around Talking." Hollywood Jesus 15 May 2004. 2 July 2004 [http://www. hollywoodjesus.com/lord_of_the_rings_interview_05.htm].

Boyens, Philippa and Fran Walsh. Interview with Jeffrey Overstreet, et al. Looking Closer 2003. 2 July 2004 [http://promontoryartists/lookingcloser/movie%20reviews/Q-Z/returnoftheking-franphilippa.htm].

Clouse, R. G. "Christian Humanism." Believe Religious Information Source. Oct. 21, 2002 [mb-soft.com/believe/txn/chrishum.htm].

Columbia World of Quotations, The. Columbia University Press, 1996. Online Edition Bartleby.com, 2001. 2 July 2004 [www.bartleby.com].

Fellowship of the Ring, The. Dir. Peter Jackson. Perf. Ian McKellen, Elijah Wood, Viggo Mortensen. 2001. DVD. New Line Home Video, 2002.

Fellowship of the Ring, The. Special Extended Edition. Dir. Peter Jackson. Perf. Ian McKellen, Elijah Wood, Viggo Mortensen.

2002. DVD. New Line Home Video, 2002.

"Film-maker Leni Riefenstahl dies." BBC News, World Edition, 9 Sep. 2003. 2 July 2004 [http://news.bbc.co.uk/2/hi/entertainment/3093154.stm].

Fox, James J. "Natural Law." The Catholic Encyclopedia. Volume 9. New York: Robert Appleton Company, 1910. 15 vols. Online Edition: Kevin Knight, 1999. Oct. 21, 2002 [www.newadvent.org/cathen/09076a.htm].

Hearts of Darkness, A Filmmaker's Apocalypse. Dir. Fax Bahr, with George Hickenlooper. Perf. Francis Ford Coppola, Martin Sheen, Dennis Hopper. American Zoetrope 1991. Videocassette. Paramount Pictures, 1992.

Holy Bible. King James Version (KJV). Electronic Edition. Quickverse for Windows 3.0d. Craig Rairdin and Parsons Technology Inc., 1992–1994.

Holy Bible. New International Version (NIV). Electronic Edition. Quickverse for Windows 3.0d. Craig Rairdin and Parsons Technology Inc., 1992–1994.

Holy Bible. New American Standard Version (NASB). The Lockman Foundation, 1960–1988. Electronic Edition. Quickverse for Windows 3.0d. Craig Rairdin and Parsons Technology Inc., 1992–1994.

Jackson, Peter. Interview with Greg Wright, et al. "The Horse's Mouth." Hollywood Jesus 15 April 2004. 2 July 2004 [http://www.hollywoodjesus.com/lord_of_the_rings_intervie w_04.htm].

Jackson, Peter. Interview with Jeffrey Overstreet, et al. Looking Closer 2003. 2 July 2004 [http://promontoryartists/looking closer/movie%20reviews/Q-Z/returnofthekingjackson.htm].

Jackson, Peter. Unpublished interview with David Bruce, et al. New Line Cinema, December 2004. Audio CD. 2 July 2004.

Kemerling, Garth. "Humanism." A Dictionary of Philosophical Terms and Names. Philosophy Pages, 1997–2002. Oct. 21,

Bibliography

2002 [www.philosophypages.com/dy/h9.htm#huma].

Kohl, Benjamin G. "Humanism." Believe Religious Information Source. Oct. 21, 2002 [mb-soft.com/believe/txn/chrishum. htm].

Meeter, Henry P. [henry.meeter@t-online.de]. "RE: Relationship to Lewis …" Private e-mail message to Greg Wright, [hjpastorgreg@hotmail.com]. 5 September 2003.

Moore, Michael. Interview with Harlan Jacobson. "Michael and Me." Film Comment November–December 1989: pp. 16–26.

Overland, Brian. [Briano2u@aol.com]. "Re: October LOTR Feature at Hollywood Jesus." Private e-mail message to Greg Wright, [hjpastorgreg@hotmail.com]. 15 October 2003.

Peterson, Eugene. The Message. Colorado Springs: Navpress, 2002.

Return of the King Digital Press Kit, The. Insert. New Line Cinema, 2003.

Return of the King, The. Dir. Arthur Rankin, Jr. and Jules Bass. Perf. Orson Bean, John Huston. Rankin/Bass Productions 1980. DVD. Warner Home Video, 2001.

Return of the King, The. Dir. Peter Jackson. Perf. Ian McKellen, Elijah Wood, Viggo Mortensen. New Line Cinema 2003. DVD. New Line Home Video, 2004.

Return of the King, The. Trailer. New Line Cinema, 2003. 2 July 2004 [http://www.lordoftherings.net/trailer_rotk_trailer_sm all.html].

Shore, Howard. Unpublished interview with David Bruce, et al. New Line Cinema, December 2004. Audio CD. 2 July 2004.

Simpson, James B. ed. Simpson's Contemporary Quotations. Boston & New York: Houghton Mifflin and Company, 1988. Online Edition Bartleby.com, 2001. 2 July 2004 [www.bartleby.com].

Sragow, Michael. "Francis Ford Coppola." salon.com, 19 Oct. 1999. 2 July 2004 [http://archive.salon.com/people/bc/1999/10/19/coppola/index1.html].

Stone, Oliver. Interview with Gavin Smith. "The camera for me is an actor." Film Comment January–February 1994: pp. 26–29, 37–43.

Tarkington, Booth. Growth. New York: Doubleday, Page & Company, 1927.

---. Some Old Portraits. New York: Doubleday, Doran & Company, 1939.

Tolkien, J. R. R. The Fellowship of the Ring. 2nd ed. Boston: Houghton Mifflin Company, 1965.

---. The Hobbit. Boston: Houghton Mifflin Company, 1966.

---. Letters. Ed. Humphrey Carpenter. Boston & New York: Houghton Mifflin Company, 2000.

---. Morgoth's Ring: The Later Silmarillion, Part One. Ed. Christopher Tolkien. The History of Middle-earth. Vol. 10. Boston & New York: Houghton Mifflin Company, 1993. 12 vols.

---. The Return of the King. 2nd ed. Boston: Houghton Mifflin Company, 1965.

---. The Silmarillion. Ed. Christopher Tolkien. Boston: Houghton Mifflin Company, 1977.

---. The Tolkien Reader. New York: Ballantine Books, 1966.

---. The Two Towers. 2nd ed. Boston: Houghton Mifflin Company, 1965.

---. Unfinished Tales. Ed. Christopher Tolkien. Boston: Houghton Mifflin Company, 1980.

Two Towers, The. Dir. Peter Jackson. Perf. Ian McKellen, Elijah Wood, Viggo Mortensen. 2002. DVD. New Line Home Video, 2003.

Bibliography

Wright, Greg. <u>Tolkien in Perspective</u>. Sisters, Oregon: VMI, 2003.

What Critics Are Saying About
Peter Jackson in Perspective

The "power" of Peter Jackson's *The Lord of the Rings* is the power of story. Greg Wright demonstrates that the greatest stories gain much of their strength from how they resonate in our lives, depicting our virtues and foibles at the religious, spiritual or moral levels. Wright brings to his critique a vast knowledge of Tolkien extending far beyond the adapted work, yet he is also sensitive to the demands of film craft—and from this perspective probes the decisions Jackson made in bringing the novel to his medium. The critic rightly points out that the greatest departures from the novel's Christian spirit occur at junctures such as Aragorn's "no mercy" cry at Helm's Deep rather than through the more obvious changes to Tolkien's story.

As the majority of these essays were originally posted on the highly popular HollywoodJesus.com website, *Peter Jackson in Perspective* is also a fascinating record of the dynamics of web criticism.

Christopher Garbowski
Maria Curie-Sklodowska University
Lublin, Poland
Author of *Recovery and Transcendence
for the Contemporary Mythmaker:
The Spiritual Dimension in the Works of JRR Tolkien.*

This book of essays is your lembas bread for the cinematic journey that is *The Lord of the Rings*. True to form, even a nibble of Wright's delicious writing will satisfy.

Amazing stuff.

Cliff Vaughn
Culture Editor, Ethics Daily

Greg Wright understands Tolkien, and he understands the power and nature of film. He writes with unmatched insight about the ways that Peter Jackson's movie trilogy alternately amplifies, mutes, and reworks Tolkien's literary tale. Wright approaches each medium with both the reverence of an enthusiast and the critical eye of an investigator. What emerges is a collection of essays that cuts to the heart of Jackson's grand interpretation. *Peter Jackson in Perspective* is an important contribution to the cultural conversation about Tolkien and film, and nobody with an interest in *The Lord of the Rings* or the intersection of faith, storytelling, and cinema should miss it.

Best commentary on the films I have read, hands-down.

Andy Rau
Managing Editor, Internet for Christians

Peter Jackson's *Lord of the Rings* trilogy has created a renaissance in epic filmmaking. Through a series of thought-provoking essays, Greg Wright captures the filmmaker's own journey to Mordor and back in *Peter Jackson in Perspective: The Power Behind Cinema's The Lord of the Rings*. This book is a must-read for Peter Jackson fans and film enthusiasts.

Michael Regina, AKA 'Xoanon'
Editor in Chief, TheOneRing.net

Wright is a master of both the Tolkien corpus and of the vast secondary literature it has spawned. In addition, Wright has honed his understanding through dialogue with *Rings* buffs worldwide in his role as Tolkien expert at HollywoodJesus.com.

Dr. Mark S. Krause
Provost, Puget Sound Christian College

ALSO BY GREG WRIGHT

TOLKIEN
IN PERSPECTIVE

SIFTING THE GOLD
FROM THE GLITTER

A Look at the Unsettling Power of
Tolkien's Mythology

Over the last fifty years, The *Lord of the Rings* has been lauded as "The Book of the Twentieth Century," and called "required reading in every Christian household." It has been attacked by literary critics and religious leaders. Its detractors are many; its defenders are legion. But there is another option.

"The chief purpose of life, for any one of us," Tolkien said, "is to increase according to our capacity our knowledge of God by all the means we have, and to be moved by it to praise and thanks."

After fifty years, it's about time to get a real handle on dealing with Tolkien's work in the way Tolkien intended. For many, *The Lord of the Rings* has proven little more than a distraction from what Tolkien called the "chief purpose of life," while still remaining a terribly neglected means of bringing others to praise and thanks.

Tolkien in Perspective: ISBN 0-9712311-6-8
VMI Publishers 2003

OTHER TOLKIEN RESOURCES BY GREG WRIGHT AT HOLLYWOODJESUS.COM

Interviews

Ian McKellen: Agendas in Middle-Earth

Elijah Wood: Carrying the Ring

Sean Astin: The Hobbit Next Door

Fran Walsh and Philippa Boyens:
A Coupla Kiwi Chicks Sitting Around Talking

Peter Jackson: The Horse's Mouth, and Other Parts

Bernard Hill: The Chivalrous King

Viggo Mortensen: What Was Medved Thinking?

John Rhys-Davies: The Wolf in Wolf's Clothing

Visual Commentary on Tolkien's **The Lord of the Rings**

The Fellowship of the Ring, Book I

The Fellowship of the Ring, Book II

The Two Towers, Book III

The Two Towers, Book IV

The Return of the King, Book V

The Return of the King, Book VI

Guest Features

"Addicted to the Ring" by Mark Sommer

"The Ring and I" by Chris Utley

"Hopeless Courage" by Loren Rosson, III

"Lost Like Gollum" by Cliff Vaughn

"The Voice of Saruman" by Brian Overland

Visit http://hollywoodjesus.com/contents_LOTR.htm